Erik Hesselberg

KON-TIKI AND I

PUBLISHER ANNE KARIN HESSELBERG

2005 Publisher Anne Karin Hesselberg.

Design and computer graphics of cover: Anne Karin Hesselberg, Rolf Wirth..

Language Adviser: Josephine Bakke.

Printing by Rolf Ottesen Grafisk produksjon, Oslo, Norway.

ISBN 82 – 996559 - 1- 9

KON-TIKI
AND I

This edition of "Kon-Tiki and I" is dedicated to

Erik's children Caélou and Susanna,

my mother Liss,

my partner Rolf

and

our son Jan-Ole

ACKNOWLEDGEMENTS

I would like to express special thanks to my partner Rolf Wirth, to Josephine Bakke, to Knut Haugland and Carl Nesjar who in their different ways have contributed to this publication.

Thanks are also due to all those working at the Kon-Tiki Museum who have encouraged the republication of this book. I would like to mention Director Maja Bauge, Marketing Manager Halfdan Tangen Jr. and Ola Semm Knutsen who delights children and adults with his readings from "Kon-Tiki and I".

"The book "Kon-Tiki and I" has now been out of print for a number of years and many people have missed it! I am fond of this book which has accompanied me since childhood and I think it deserves to live on.

My father, **ERIK HESSELBERG (1914-1972),** was a colourful man with many artistic

talents. He grew up in Larvik and went to sea after finishing his schooling. He later decided to become a painter. He studied art in Germany and carried out various espionage operations for the Norwegian Resistance during the war. At the end of the war he and his wife Liss settled in Borre. It was here that one day he was asked by Thor Heyerdahl to take part in the Kon-Tiki expedition. It did not take long before my father was ready to leave with guitar and sketchbook under his arm. As the only man with a seaman`s certificate on board the raft he was appointed navigator. There was plenty of time to draw, write, carve wooden sculptures and entertain the crew with songs, guitar playing and adventure stories while on the Kon-Tiki.

After the Kon-Tiki voyage and a period of lecturing at home and abroad, he built his own sailing vessel "Tiki" and left for the Mediterranean Sea. He lived on his boat for many years off the Côte d`Azur, Corsica and Italy while he painted pictures, wrote and composed his own songs. After having sold "Tiki" he lived in the USA, Germany and Sweden for many years before returning home to Larvik. My father managed to make a living from his artwork and he carried out a number of commissioned works of art. He had among others long-standing working relationships with Pablo Picasso and Carl Nesjar. The Picasso sculpture in Kristinehamn, the statue "Sylvette" in New York and the decoration of Østermalms Torg in Stockholm provide evidence of this. He was, however, not interested in promoting himself as an artist. He wanted to be free to do things of his own choice. There was always something which attracted his curiosity and creative talent, whether it was the "Tiki game", the emergency transmitter "TAB", sound experiments, language studies, history, the Gingko tree, the unique world of moss or a plan to landscape an arboretum. He died in Larvik only 58 years old. He donated his collection of songs to the University of Oslo.

KON-TIKI AND I was first published in Norwegian in 1949. My father had already started the text and sketches for the book while on the raft. The book soon became popular all over the world and it was translated into 15 languages. The book is a lively and highly personal account of the Kon-Tiki expedition and life on and under the balsa raft.

The book has now been republished! I wish all readers, children and adults, an adventurous voyage from Kirkebakken Borre to the Polynesian Islands..

Best wishes   *Anne Karin Hesselberg*

ERIK HESSELBERG

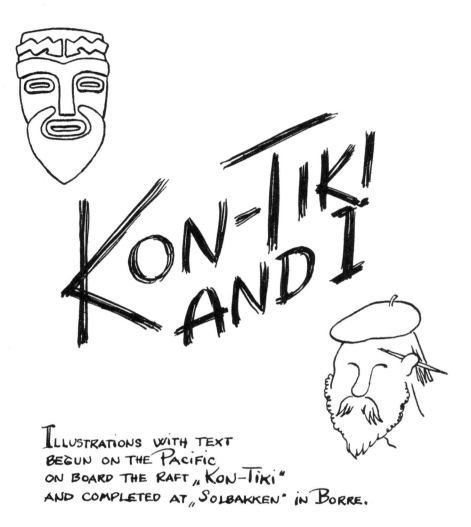

KON-TIKI AND I

ILLUSTRATIONS WITH TEXT
BEGUN ON THE PACIFIC
ON BOARD THE RAFT „KON-TIKI"
AND COMPLETED AT „SOLBAKKEN" IN BORRE.

DEDICATED TO MY ONLY WIFE

Liss

WHO HAD TO SIT AT HOME
AND MIND THE CHILD

Anne Karin

WHILE I WAS HAVING
STRANGE EXPERIENCES.

THIS IS MY ONLY WIFE, AS I SAW
HER IN MY MIND'S EYE - -

AND THIS IS MY ONLY
DAUGHTER

THESE TWO I LEFT BEHIND - - - - -

-- AND „SOLBAKKEN".

THAT IS THE NAME OF THE HOUSE WE LIVE IN. IT STANDS CLOSE TO BORRE CHURCH AND LOOKS LIKE THIS.

I LEFT IT, LISS AND ANNE KARIN, PIUS THE CAT, CASA NOVA THE COCK, AND FIVE HENS. THE HENS ARE CALLED SOFIE, AMALIE, CHRISTINE, AGATE AND GERD; GERD IS FAIRLY YOUNG, THE OTHERS COULD QUITE WELL BE HER AUNTS, BUT THEY ARE ALWAYS PECKING AND HUSTLING HER.

OTHERWISE ALL AT „SOLBAKKEN" ARE GOOD FRIENDS, AND IT WAS SAD TO SAY GOOD-BYE TO THEM.

GERD

ONE COLD MORNING IN FEBRUARY I WALKED TO BORRE STATION TO TRAVEL TO LIMA IN THE COUNTRY CALLED PERU - ON THE OTHER SIDE OF THE ATLANTIC, ON THE OTHER SIDE OF SOUTH AMERICA.

PIUS WENT WITH ME FOR A BIT OF THE WAY.

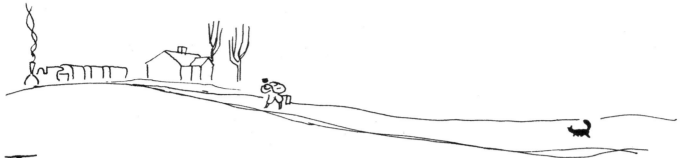

THE PORTER-CUM-BOOKING CLERK GUNDERSEN DIDN'T KNOW WHERE LIMA WAS, BUT HE GAVE ME A TICKET TO OSLO.

SO I GOT INTO A TRAIN ON THE VESTFOLD RAILWAY, AND THAT WAS THE REAL START OF MY PREHISTORIC JOURNEY. THE VESTFOLD RAILWAY WAS ALREADY A PREHISTORIC CHAPTER IN ITSELF.

" WHERE DID YOU SAY YOU WERE GOING — TO LIMA? WHERE THE HELL'S THAT? "

IT LOOKED LIKE THIS WHEN I WAS A LITTLE BOY, —

— — IT LOOKED LIKE THIS WHEN I WENT TO LIMA, AND IT WILL CERTAINLY LOOK LIKE THIS WHEN I COME BACK. MY FATHER SAID THAT WHEN HE WAS YOUNG THERE WAS A LOT OF TALK ABOUT CONVERTING IT TO BROAD GAUGE.

THE WOMAN WHO SAT OPPOSITE ME SLEPT ALL THE WAY TO DRAMMEN.

THE LITTLE THIN MAN HAD BEEN TO TÖNSBERG TO SEE HIS SICK WIFE, AND THERE WAS A CHAP IN A CARDIGAN WHO SAID IT WAS A COLD DAY.

THESE WERE SOME OF MY FIRST TRAVELLING COMPANIONS ON MY WAY TO LIMA.

THE CHAP IN THE CARDIGAN GOT OUT AT NYKIRKE AND THE LITTLE THIN MAN AT HOLMESTRAND.

THEN A FELLOW GOT IN WHO KNEW A MAN WHO KNEW A FRIEND OF MINE. HE TALKED ALL THE WAY TO OSLO. HE HAD BEEN IN ENGLAND DURING THE WAR AND HAD GROWN A LITTLE MOUSTACHE.

I HAD A LOT OF THINGS TO DO IN OSLO, BUT FIRST I WENT TO FRED OLSEN'S OFFICE TO FIND OUT WHEN THE „LAURITZ SWENSON" WOULD SAIL. 3 P.M. SHARP, SOMEONE SAID. 7.30 P.M., SAID SOMEONE WHO HAD IT FROM THE SKIPPER HIMSELF. AT 8 NEXT MORNING THE „LAURITZ SWENSON" SAILED FOR PANAMA WITH ME ON BOARD.

I WANTED TO INSURE MY LIFE FOR 50,000 KRONER, BUT NOBODY WOULD, NOT EVEN FOR 50 ÖRE. THIS IS WHAT THE INSURANCE AGENT LOOKED LIKE WHEN I HAD REACHED THE CLIMAX IN THE STORY OF MY PRE-INCA LIFE.

– – „AND WHEN YOU'VE GOT ON BOARD A WOODEN RAFT AND DRIFTED ACROSS THE PACIFIC IN IT, WHAT THEN?"

THE „LAURITZ SWENSON" IS A MOTOR SHIP RUNNING BETWEEN NORWAY AND CALIFORNIA. SHE IS A NICE BOAT, WITH A NICE SKIPPER AND NICE PEOPLE.

My fellow-passengers were nice too, so I have only pleasant memories of the ship.

The whole Oslo Fjord was full of ice, but the „Lauritz" ploughed her way through with swank and style.

Just then it occurred to me that I had forgotten my bathing drawers.

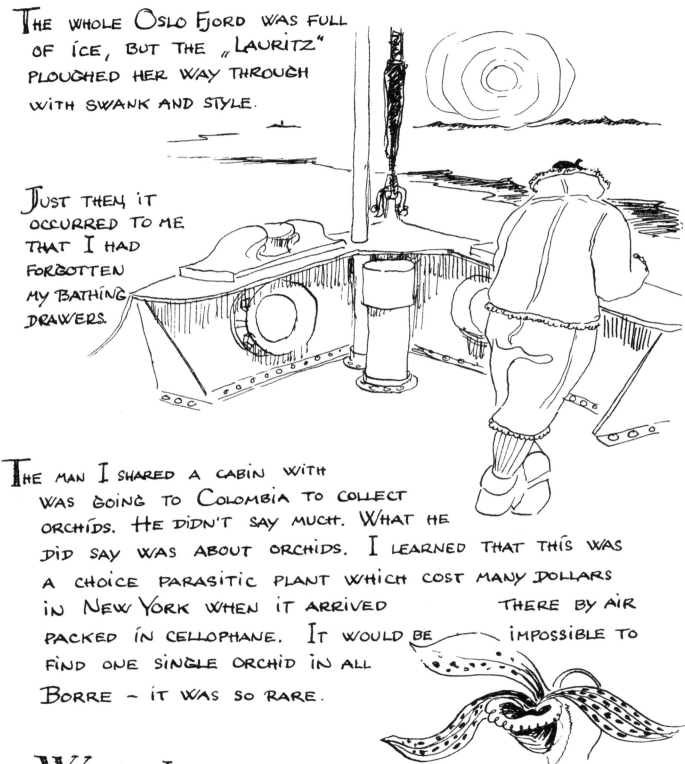

The man I shared a cabin with was going to Colombia to collect orchids. He didn't say much. What he did say was about orchids. I learned that this was a choice parasitic plant which cost many dollars in New York when it arrived there by air packed in cellophane. It would be impossible to find one single orchid in all Borre - it was so rare.

West of Ireland we had some dirty weather – –

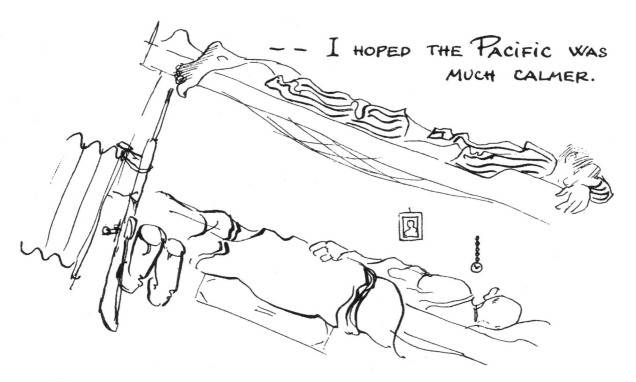

-- I HOPED THE PACIFIC WAS MUCH CALMER.

THE OTHER PASSENGERS WERE 10 DIFFERENT TYPES OF LADIES, AND A DENTIST A. BÖHN WHO WAS A MAN AND

LARS OFTEDAL WHO WAS A BOY.

HERE ARE A COUPLE OF THE LADIES—

- AND HERE IS THE MAN WHO WAS GOING TO COLLECT ORCHIDS IN THE INTERIOR OF COLOMBIA. HE PROPOSED THAT I SHOULD STAY IN THE JUNGLE WITH HIM INSTEAD OF SITTING ON A RAFT IN THE PACIFIC.

As to great events on the voyage, it can be stated that the first officer had a son by wireless, and that a bathing pool was rigged up on DECK. I borrowed the skipper's bathing drawers. Then one day a hazy coast appeared RIGHT AHEAD.

It was Panama, and 25 days HAD PASSED SINCE we left the ice of the OSLO FJORD — THAT ice must have been still there

At Cristobal, at the entrance to the Panama Canal, I went ashore. The orchid man did the same. The „Lauritz" lay there for a couple of hours, then she pushed her nose into the canal and was off. There we stood.

We were quickly surrounded by Customs officials, who triumphantly confiscated the orchid man's gun. When they took away the gun he was much distressed and looked appealingly at me, for he could speak neither English nor Spanish, but was otherwise a brave man. In my opinion, he was close up to the bravest of foreigners.

I EXPLAINED AS WELL AS I COULD THAT HE
WAS GOING TO USE THE GUN FOR ORCHID-HUNTING AND NOT
TO SHOOT AT THE PRESIDENT OF THE COUNTRY. I KEPT ON
WITH THIS TILL THEY SAID THAT WE MUST TALK TO „ EL
COMANDANTE". HE LIVED IN A GUARD-HOUSE AND WAS
INTERRUPTED IN HIS GAME OF DICE, BUT ALL THE SAME
HE LISTENED PATIENTLY TO WHAT WE HAD TO SAY. THEN
HE LISTENED TO WHAT THE CUSTOMS PARTY HAD TO SAY, —
TO THE MAN WHO DISCOVERED THE GUN ON THE FLOWER
MAN'S SHOULDER, TO THE MAN WHO DEMANDED THAT THE GUN

SHOULD BE EXAMINED AND TO THE MAN
WHO RECEIVED THE GUN AND SAID
THAT NOW IT WAS CONFISCATED.
EL COMANDANTE THREW DICE AT
INTERVALS AND LOOKED PENSIVE.
WHEN QUIET WAS RESTORED, HE SAID
IT WAS A MATTER FOR THE POLICE.

WELL, WE WENT TO THE POLICE
AND WAITED ABOUT AN HOUR FOR A
FELLOW NAMED GONZALES.
NOBODY KNEW WHERE GONZALES
WAS, BUT THEN A MAN CALLED LOPEZ
CAME AND SAID THAT GONZALES WAS
WITH MADAME RODRIGUEZ WHO KEPT
THE IMPERIALE HOTEL JUST DOWN
THE STREET.

CAFE   10¢
CAFE CON LECHE 15¢
HELADO 20¢
HELADO DE
   PLATANOS

WELL, WE WENT TO
MADAME RODRIGUEZ
JUST DOWN THE STREET
TO MEET GONZALES WHO
KNEW ABOUT OUR CASE.
BUT THEN WE WERE SO HOT
AND TIRED THAT WE HAD TO
GO INTO A PLACE AND EAT
ICES.

GONZALES

MADAME RODRÍGUEZ

WE FOUND GONZALES IN MADAME RODRÍGUEZ' OFFICE. SEVERAL DUBIOUS LOOKING PEOPLE WERE SITTING THERE, AND THERE WAS A MARKED SILENCE WHEN WE WENT IN. GONZALES SAID IT WAS A MATTER FOR THE CUSTOMS, BUT WE GOT HIM TO SIGN A STATEMENT THAT HE GONZALES AND THEREBY THE POLICE HAD NO OBJECTION TO NILS PEDERSEN DE DROEBAK, NORUEGA, GETTING HIS GUN BACK WHEN HE LEFT THE REPUBLIC OF PANAMA. I ASKED RODRÍGUEZ IF WE COULD STAY AT THE HOTEL. THERE WAS DEAD SILENCE AGAIN AND THE MEN LOOKED AT US AND FROM US TO MADAME. SHE LOOKED AT US AND FROM US TO THE MEN. I HAD A VERY STRONG FEELING THAT THE WHOLE CROWD WAS A GANG AND THAT SOME SHADY BUSINESS WAS GOING ON IN THE HOTEL -- WHITE SLAVE TRAFFIC AND PERHAPS EVEN WORSE THINGS.

GONZALES WAS OBVIOUSLY THE RINGLEADER.

We asked if there was any white slave traffic in the town. No, – they said, and exchanged looks again. Pedersen asked me in our room afterwards if one could buy whites on the black market — but of course he was only trying to be funny. It ended by our being entered in the hotel register as „Turistos Noruegos", and then we went to fetch our packs and suitcases and all our parcels.

Pedersen thought that Gonzales was a nice chap and that Madame Rodriguez was awfully kind.

After this we had to have more ices.

In the evening we wanted to see some Latin-American national life, for Pedersen had hardly been out of Dröbak before. A ceaseless stream of music issued from a place called „El Jacaré"(the Crocodile). We went in, but there was not a soul to be seen, only a gaudy machine

PLAYING WITH A DEAFENING NOISE AND A CROCODILE HANGING FROM THE CEILING. RED LIGHT SHONE FROM THE CROCODILE'S EYES.

NOT TILL ABOUT MIDNIGHT DID THE NATIONAL LIFE BEGIN, WITH DANCING AND A REAL BAND »———————→

IN SOME OF THE DANCES PEOPLE JUST STOOD STILL AND WRIGGLED THEIR BEHINDS, AND IN OTHERS THEY MADE A FEW CURIOUS SNAKE-LIKE MOVEMENTS WITH LITTLE JERKS NOW AND THEN. PEDERSEN WAS MOST INTERESTED IN THE CROCODILE UP ON THE CEILING; HE WANTED TO KNOW WHO HAD SHOT IT.

THE CROCODILE STARED AT US ALL THE TIME.

WE CAME HOME TO THE IMPERIALE LATE AT NIGHT AND TIRED. A LIGHT SHONE FROM RODRIGUEZ' OFFICE, AND I REMEMBERED MY RESOLUTION TO KEEP A SHARP EYE ON THE SHADY CUSTOMERS. I LOOKED THROUGH THE KEYHOLE. THERE SAT GONZALES WITH RODRIGUEZ ON HIS LAP ---. THEN I SHOOK HANDS WITH PEDERSEN AND WISHED HIM A GOOD JOURNEY AND PLENTY OF ORCHIDS. I HAVE NOT SEEN HIM SINCE.

A PLANE WAS GOING TO LIMA NEXT MORNING FROM A PLACE CALLED BALBOA. IT LAY ON THE PACIFIC SIDE

AND I WENT THERE BY A TRAIN
WHICH RAN ALONG THE PANAMA CANAL.
I SAW MANY PICTURESQUE LITTLE SCENES
FROM THE NATIVES' LIFE, LIKE THE ONE
ON THE PREVIOUS PAGE.

THIS IS WHAT THE SHIPS ON THE PANAMA CANAL LOOKED LIKE SEEN FROM THE TRAIN.

THE PLANE WAS LATE, SO I HAD A FEW HOURS AT PANAMA CITY, THE CAPITAL OF THE COUNTRY. IN FRONT OF THE CATHEDRAL I MET A MAN WHO WANTED TO SELL A REAL GOLD RING INCREDIBLY CHEAPLY.

HE LOOKED LIKE THIS AND HAD SEVERAL RINGS IN HIS POCKET.

THERE WAS A LOT OF GOLD INSIDE THE CATHEDRAL TOO - IMAGES WITH GLASS EYES AND REAL HUMAN HAIR AND WITH PAPER FLOWERS IN THEIR HANDS.

THE MAIN STREET LOOKS SOMETHING LIKE THIS.

JUST IN THE FRONT OF THE GREAT GOLDEN ALTAR WAS A 10-CENT
AUTOMAT - - „FOR POSTCARDS"

BORRE CHURCH IS MUCH NICER, I THINK,
ALTHOUGH IT COULD EASILY GET INTO
THE SACRISTY HERE.

POSTCARDS
PUT A DIME
IN THE SLOT
AND YOU'LL
GET
A
NICE POSTCARD

THE PLANE WAS A GREAT SILVER BIRD
CALLED; *Panagra 5077*

I THOUGHT THOSE TWO 7S WERE GOOD.
THE DOOR IN THE FUSELAGE WAS MUCH BIGGER
THAN THOSE ON THE VESTFOLD RAILWAY.

INSIDE IT LOOKED LIKE A CROSS BETWEEN A BARBER'S SHOP
AND A HOSPITAL.

I SAW A SHIP ON THE PACIFIC
AND THOUGHT OF
THE RAFT - - WHAT
IT WOULD LOOK LIKE
FROM A PLANE.
I SAW BROWN RIVERS
AND A CARPET OF
GREEN JUNGLE IN
ECUADOR. I SAW
THE CORRUGATED
IRON ROOFS IN
GUAYAQUIL GLITTERING
IN THE SUN. I SAW THE
MOON SHINE OVER THE
DESOLATE COASTAL DESERT
OF NORTHERN PERU, AND
AT LAST LIMA LIKE A
BRILLIANT JEWEL DOWN
IN THE DARKNESS. THE FLIGHT
WAS OVER AFTER 8 HOURS AND
THE GREAT BIRD DESCENDED OVER
LIMATAMBO, THE AIRFIELD OF LIMA,
THE CAPITAL OF PERU.

SIMON BOLIVAR MUST HAVE BEEN TREMENDOUSLY POPULAR IN SOUTH AMERICA. A LOT OF THINGS ARE CALLED AFTER HIM — INCLUDING THE HOTEL I PUT UP AT IN LIMA. IT TOOK UP A WHOLE BLOCK IN THE PLAZA SAN MARTIN. MADAME RODRIGUEZ' PLACE AT CRISTOBAL WAS JUST A STABLE COMPARED TO IT. NONE OF THE OTHER HOTELS IN LIMA ARE AS LARGE AS THE BOLIVAR. HERMAN WAS STAYING THERE AND HE IS ONE OF THE KON-TIKI CROWD. HERMAN TOLD ME THAT HIS HEAD HAD BEEN THE WRONG WAY ROUND FOR A TIME BUT IT WAS THE RIGHT WAY ROUND NOW, AND THAT I MUST LOOK OUT FOR BIG WAVES ON THE BATHING BEACH OUTSIDE LIMA — THEY HAD TWISTED HERMAN'S HEAD ROUND. THERE WERE ONLY THREE KON-TIKI MEN IN LIMA THEN — HERMAN, BENGT AND I. APART FROM THE PRESIDENT AND SOME OF THE MINISTERS THERE WERE NOT MANY PEOPLE WHO KNEW ABOUT KON-TIKI, — BUT SOON ALL LIMA KNEW, AND ALL PERU.

Ciudad de Lima

THE OLD TOWN OF LIMA WAS FOUNDED BY PIZARRO IN 1535

← BENGT EMMERIK DANIELSSON

But 1500 years ago there were many in Peru who knew Kon-Tiki. The sun was the greatest of the gods in those days, and Kon-Tiki stood between the sun and the people. Indian tradition says that he was white-skinned and had a beard.

Successors of his race built great cities in the wild Andes mountains. To-day they are ruins. Only mountain Indians wander about alone with their llamas.

The Indians are brown and have no beards, so Kon-Tiki must have belonged to a white race which has long been extinct in South America. Tradition has it that the city on Lake Titicaca in which Kon-Tiki lived was attacked by Indians, but that Kon-Tiki managed to escape to the coast with some friends. There they embarked on balsa-wood rafts and disappeared across the Pacific — to go home to the sun, the legend says.

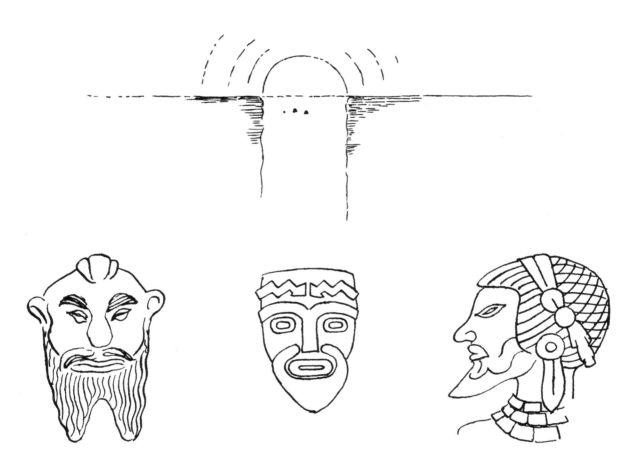

Whether Kon-Tiki looked like this — or like this — or like this it is hard to say. But all these bearded faces in stone and clay were dug up in America.

1500 years passed without anyone giving another thought to it, but then Thor Heyerdahl began to think about Kon-Tiki — and that was no wonder because he was studying the problem of the Polynesians' origin — a problem which has turned many ethnologists' hair grey.

THE POLYNESIANS LIVE ON A NUMBER OF SMALL ISLANDS ROUGHLY IN THE MIDDLE OF THE PACIFIC. THEY ARE HANDSOME AND LIGHTSKINNED AND BELONG TO AN UNKNOWN MIXED RACE. THERE ARE MANY CURIOUS MONOLITHS ON THE ISLANDS WHICH BEAR WITNESS TO A HIGH CULTURE WHICH ONCE WAS THERE. ON EASTER ISLAND HUNDREDS OF HUGE STONE FACES STAND STARING OUT OVER THE SEA. THEY HAVE LONG EARS AND NOSES. SOME OF THE NOSES ARE NEARLY 10 FT. LONG, BUT THEY ARE ON FACES WHICH ARE NEARLY 40 FT. LONG FROM THE THROAT TO THE TOP OF THE STONE CAP. ON THE OTHER ISLANDS THERE ARE GIANT GODS, BOTH STANDING AND LYING.

HERE IS ONE LYING ON HIS STOMACH.

ONE OF THE GODS IN POLYNESIAN LEGEND IS CALLED TIKI. HE WAS THE GREATEST OF THE GODS ON SOME OF THE ISLANDS. HE WAS SON OF THE SUN AND LED HIS PEOPLE OUT INTO THE PACIFIC.

THOR HEYERDAHL LIVED ON THESE ISLANDS FOR A TIME, AND HEARD A LOT OF TALK ABOUT TIKI FROM AN OLD CANNIBAL CALLED TEI TETUA. BUT HE HAD GIVEN UP EATING PEOPLE WHEN THOR MET HIM. THEN HE JUST SAT AND CHEWED SUGAR-CANE.. EVENTUALLY THOR HEYERDAHL BECAME SO INTERESTED IN THE POLYNES-IANS' ORIGIN THAT HE DEVOTED HIMSELF WHOLLY TO THE STUDY OF THIS QUESTION. HE WORKED AT IT FOR MANY YEARS AND CAME TO THE CONCLUSION THAT THEY ORIGINATED IN SOUTH AMERICA AND THAT KON-TIKI FROM PERU AND TIKI IN POLYNESIA WERE THE SAME PERSON.

KON-TIKI WENT HOME NOT TO THE SUN, BUT TO POLYNESIA WITH HIS BALSA RAFTS. THOR HEYERDAHL WAS SO SURE OF IT THAT HE WROTE A THESIS AND PUT IT TO THE AMERICAN SPECIALISTS, FOR THEY WERE THE PEOPLE WHO COUNTED IN THIS MATTER. BUT NONE OF THEM BELIEVED IN THIS THEORY. THEY WOULD NOT BELIEVE THAT A PRIMITIVE BALSA RAFT COULD CARRY MEN 4300 MILES ACROSS THE OPEN SEA.

"THEN I'LL PROVE THAT IT'S POSSIBLE" SAID THOR HEYERDAHL.

POLYNESIA AND AMERICA A STUDY IN CULTURE RELATIONS

BY THOR HEYERDAHL

THAT WAS WHAT WE WERE IN LIMA FOR - TO BUILD A RAFT OF BALSA WOOD FROM OLD SPANISH DRAWINGS AND CROSS THE SEA AS KON-TIKI HAD DONE. THE HUMBOLDT CURRENT, THE SOUTH EQUATORIAL CURRENT AND THE S.E. TRADE WIND WOULD HELP US TO CROSS AS THEY HAD HELPED KON-TIKI.

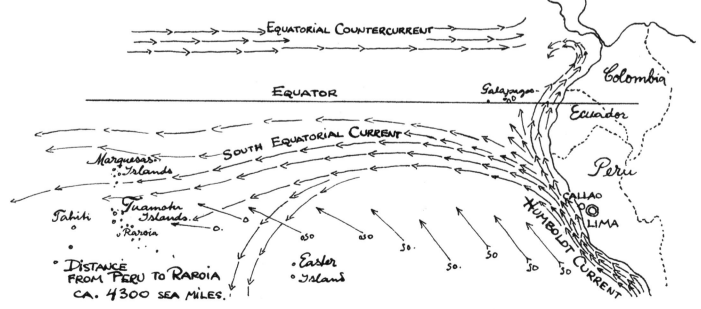

Equatorial Countercurrent

Equator

Colombia

Galapagos

Ecuador

South Equatorial Current

Peru

Marquesas Islands

CALLAO

Tahiti

Tuamotu Islands

LIMA

Raroia

Humbolt Current

Easter Island

Distance from Peru to Raroia ca. 4300 sea miles.

Thor and Herman got nine balsa-logs from the jungle in Ecuador. Balsa is a light kind of wood, but not so easy to cut. Nevertheless they cut the trees down themselves and tied them together with lianas down on a little stream which ran through the jungle.

Then they sat on the top of the cargo and drifted downstream all the way to the port of Guayaquil.

Then the logs came by cargo boat to Callao, the port of Lima. They were lying on a railway truck there when I appeared on the scene. Then Torstein came from New York one day and after him Thor and Knut.
The Kon-Tiki party was assembled
Here they are with their Christian names:

Thor Heyerdahl
Herman Watzinger
Bengt Emmerik Danielsson
Knut Haugland
Torstein Raaby
and
I myself, who stand 6 ft. 4 inches above sea level, am easily recognisable.

Knut   Herman   Thor   Self   Bengt   Torstein

LOS EXPEDICIONARIOS

or

LOS TRIPULANTES DE LA "BALSA"

As the Lima papers called us.
Gerd Vold was secretary to the expedition all the time. She looks something like this, but is much prettier. She gave us excellent help, and the papers called her the raft's godmother.

-- La madrina de la balsa.

THE PRESIDENT OF THE COUNTRY GAVE US PERMISSION TO BUILD OUR RAFT IN THE NAVAL HARBOUR, ARSENAL NAVAL.
THE PRESIDENT HAD A QUEER NAME, WE THOUGHT.
HE WAS CALLED:
ALTENTAMENTE, EXCELLENTE PRESIDENTE BUSTAMENTE.
BUT NO ONE IN PERU THOUGHT IT AT ALL QUEER. THE LAST WAS HIS NAME. ALL THE REST WERE TITLES.
THE PRESIDENT WAS KIND ENOUGH ACTUALLY TO LEND US ONE OF HIS CARS AS WELL.
THERE WERE A LOT OF KIND PEOPLE IN PERU. "
¡SKAAL, VIKINGOS DEL "KON-TIKI"! THEY SAID, AND LIKED" TO HAVE US AROUND IN THEIR PARTIES AND GAVE US AS GOOD A TIME AS THEY COULD. BUT THAT WAS NOT WHY WE TOOK 3 MONTHS TO BUILD THE RAFT. NO, IT WASN'T SO EASY TO BUILD RAFTS IN PERU.

THE GUARD OF THE PRESIDENT

AT THE BEGINNING A MAN CALLED ALFREDO HIMENEZ FOUND US SOME RATINGS TO HELP WITH THE COLLAR-WORK. BUT WE SOON TOOK OVER THE WORK OURSELVES.
WE LAID THE NINE LOGS SIDE BY SIDE LIKE ORGANPIPES AND LASHED EACH LOG TO ITS NEIGHBOUR WITH ORDINARY HEMP ROPES AND WOODEN PEGS. WE LASHED A FEW SMALLER LOGS CROSSWAYS ON TOP OF THE NINE. THIS COMPLETED THE HULL, BUT THERE WERE NO PRETTY LINES TO BE SEEN ANYWHERE, SO I DON'T THINK ONE CAN CALL A RAFT "SHE".
WE COULD NOT USE IRON IN THIS VESSEL, FOR NOTHING OF THE KIND WAS KNOWN IN AMERICA BEFORE COLUMBUS.

ON THE TOP OF THE CROSS-WISE LOGS WE LAID HALF-ROUNDED AND PLAITED BAMBOOS AS A KIND OF DECK.

MARINEROS

ALFREDO HIMENEZ

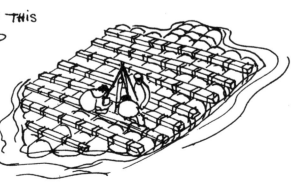

← CENTREBOARD
TO STEER WITH

THEN WE BUILT A CABIN OF BAMBOOS AND LATTICE-WORK. THE ROOF CONSISTED OF THIN BAMBOOS AND BANANA LEAVES. THIS CABIN MIGHT JUST AS WELL HAVE BEEN IN THE MIDDLE OF THE JUNGLE. INSIDE IT WAS NOT EXACTLY A DANCE-HALL. AT SEA WE LAY IN IT THE SARDINE SYSTEM. THE MAST LOOKED LIKE THIS AND WAS OF MANGO WOOD WHICH IS SO HEAVY AND HARD THAT IT SINKS IN WATER.

Según Benzoni, autor italiano del siglo XVII en esta balsa los peruanos recorrieron las costas del mar Pacífico.

WE MADE A SAIL ABOUT 13 FT. BY 16 FT. TOO, AND I PAINTED A KON-TIKI HEAD ON IT. AT LAST THE RAFT LAY THERE AND WAS SUCH A STRANGE CRAFT THAT A CROWD OF PEOPLE CAME TO STARE AT IT EVERY DAY. IT LOOKED LIKE A QUEER CONTRAPTION LASHED TOGETHER WITH ROPE-ENDS.

THE OLD SPANISH DRAWINGS WE USED AS MODELS REPRESENTED BIGGER RAFTS THAN THIS. OUR RAFT WAS AS EXACT A COPY AS POSSIBLE.

WE STOWED THE PROVISIONS UNDER THE MATS.

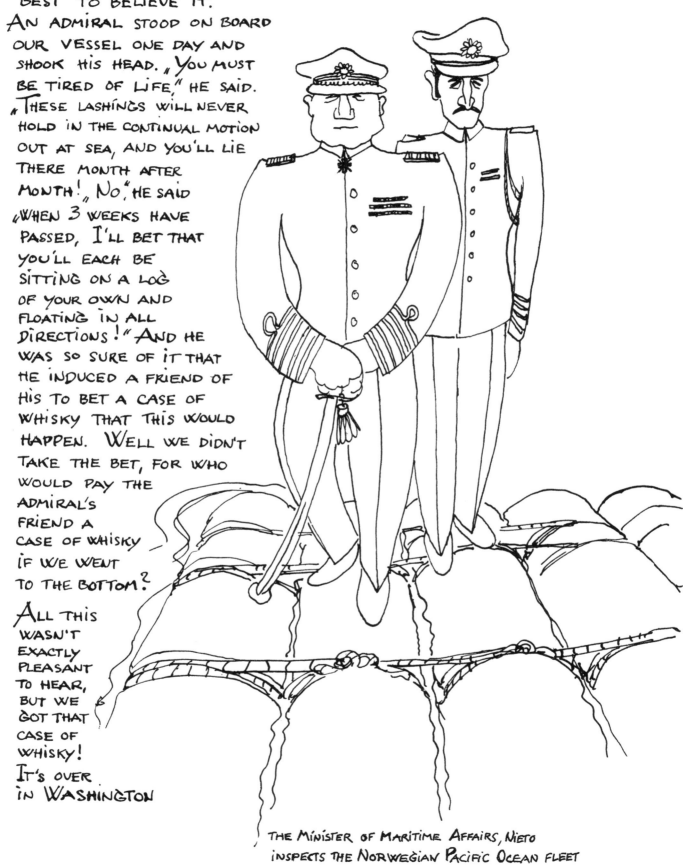

But there were not many who believed things would go well. It was surely only we six „tripulantes" who did our best to believe it.

An admiral stood on board our vessel one day and shook his head. „You must be tired of life," he said. „These lashings will never hold in the continual motion out at sea, and you'll lie there month after month! „No", he said „When 3 weeks have passed, I'll bet that you'll each be sitting on a log of your own and floating in all directions!" And he was so sure of it that he induced a friend of his to bet a case of whisky that this would happen. Well we didn't take the bet, for who would pay the admiral's friend a case of whisky if we went to the bottom?

All this wasn't exactly pleasant to hear, but we got that case of whisky! It's over in Washington

The Minister of Maritime Affairs, Nieto inspects the Norwegian Pacific Ocean fleet

It was much worse to listen to a fat little Norwegian skipper and his mate and boatswain. The lashings won't hold, they said, and if they _do_ hold it'll take at least a year to get to Polynesia with this contraption. But there's another thing which is wrong, said the skipper, and that's the balsa wood of the logs. Why, it's as porous as blotting paper, he said.

So when you're drifting west with the current, you'll soon find that the logs sink deeper and deeper --- and then he set out to describe what would happen then. He had imagination, and he enjoyed it, I am sure, for he described how the water would rise above our ankles and up over our calves, over our knees and stomachs — how the cabin would disappear and we would have the water up to our necks, yes, right up under our noses! I thought it sounded awful, for I am nearly a head taller than the others and if this happened I should be the last man. I already saw in my mind's eye only the tufts of my companions' hair and the fins of approaching sharks. Of Bengt Emmerik Danielsson I did not see even a tuft of hair, for he had all his hair on his chin and was bald on the top of his head.

But luckily the skipper was wrong, and those who maintained that our feet would rot were wrong too. We ourselves had, as it were, no time to be afraid. At the end we were busy day and night with all the stuff that had to be stowed on board.

None the less we made a last trip up into the Andes to savour impressions of rock and earth.

Out at sea we often thought of that trip.

We got right up to a height of 13,000 ft., though there were more people out of the car than in it

Indian women sat along the edge of the road selling silver work and carved calabashes. (a kind of gourd)

ON APRIL 27 THE RAFT WAS NAMED WITH A
COCOANUT BY GERD VOLD AND RECEIVED THE NAME
„KON-TIKI"

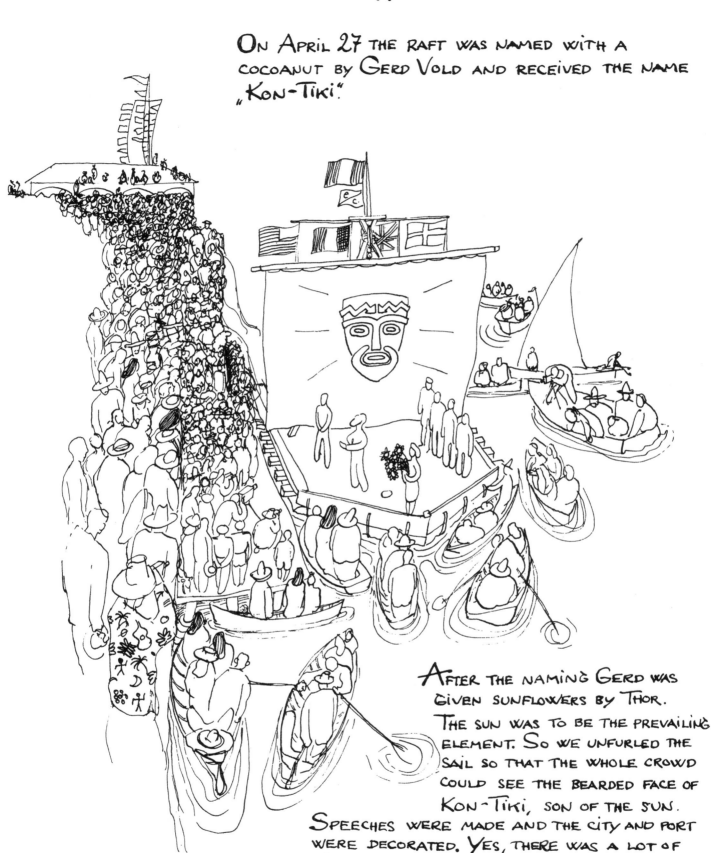

AFTER THE NAMING GERD WAS
GIVEN SUNFLOWERS BY THOR.
THE SUN WAS TO BE THE PREVAILING
ELEMENT. SO WE UNFURLED THE
SAIL SO THAT THE WHOLE CROWD
COULD SEE THE BEARDED FACE OF
KON-TIKI, SON OF THE SUN.
SPEECHES WERE MADE AND THE CITY AND PORT
WERE DECORATED. YES, THERE WAS A LOT OF
LIFE THAT DAY.

On April 28 we had got so far. Late in the afternoon Callao became black with people. Thor and a parrot stood on the nine logs surrounded by journalists and farewell presents which kind friends came lugging along. The rest of us were expected any minute. Herman was drinking a last glass of beer; Knut and Torstein were fixing up some wireless business in the town. Bengt and I were chasing round to buy a paraffin lantern and soldering paste for the wireless. But there was nothing about soldering paste in the Spanish dictionary and it wasn't so easy to explain what soldering paste was making faces and gesticulating, so it took a long time.

Soldering Paste ?

Then the tug came chugging along, long before the agreed time. A party of sailors swarmed on board the Kon-Tiki and made fast a strong hawser. Just at that moment the parrot escaped from its cage. Thor tried to stop the sailors and catch the bird at the same

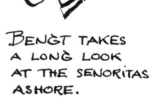

Bengt takes a long look at the senoritas ashore.

time. He only succeeded in doing the second and, amid tremendous cheering from the crowd, „La Balsa" began to move with Thor and the parrot and all the journalists on board. Thor's despairing cry „Los otros expedicionarios!!" was drowned by the cheering and it was not till well out in the harbour that the people in the tug understood that there was only one „Expedicionario" on board. When Bengt and I came down to the quay with the lantern and soldering paste, we met people on their way home. A watchman at the gate stopped us and said that there was nothing more to see now. „La Balsa" had gone. „But we're going to Polynesia with her", we said. Then he laughed loudly and barred the way still more firmly.

But we are the steward and navigator, we said. And I'm the engineer, he said, with a wink. He was clearly a natural humorist. But we were not inclined for humour just then; we pushed the watchman out of the way and hurried down to the raft's berth. There was nothing there but water and a few splinters of balsa wood. Then we saw the fair heads of Torstein and Knut in a boat with a load of people and we jumped in on top.

Out in the harbour we caught sight of the Kon-Tiki's crossed mast with a black mass under it — there were so many people on board. The first thing we had to do was to clear the deck of photographers and journalists.

In the middle of the heap we found Thor and the parrot severely battered by the Press.

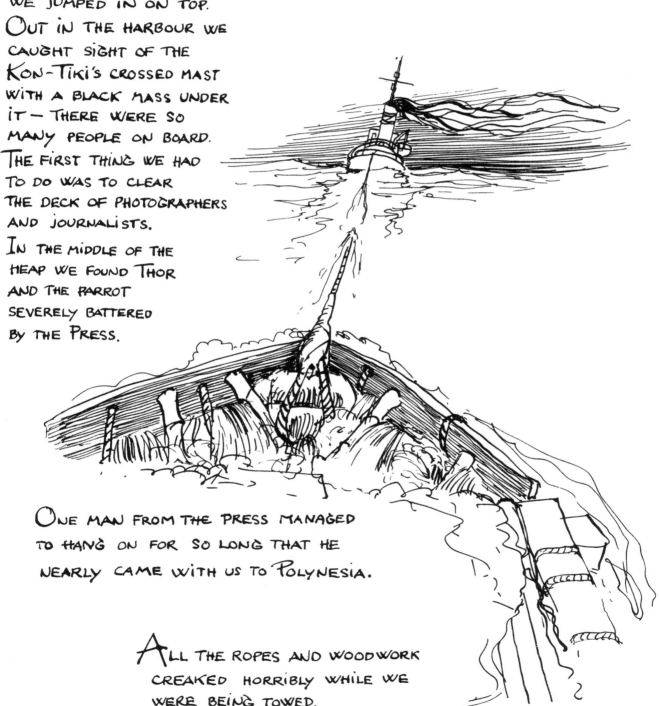

One man from the press managed to hang on for so long that he nearly came with us to Polynesia.

All the ropes and woodwork creaked horribly while we were being towed.

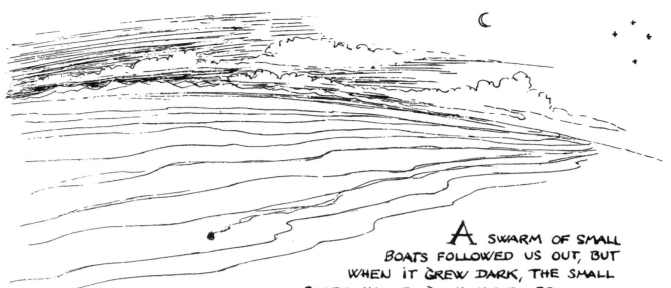

A swarm of small boats followed us out, but when it grew dark, the small boats had to go home to bed.

Next day we and the tug were alone, well beyond the island of San Lorenzo.

Then the great moment came when we cut the umbilical which still fastened us to Mother Earth. That was decisive.

It was a strange sensation to see the tug disappear and to think of the enormous distance we were to drift on our little raft – a distance of open sea as far as from Newcastle to the North Pole and back again to Newcastle.

And far, far out to sea, 4300 sea miles away, we were to strike a few small islands, as small as grains of sand – in a craft without steering gear.

These thoughts came and went through my head the first night on the real sea, while the Kon-Tiki tossed up and down, up and down. I clearly felt how the log I lay on had a mind of its own.

The next log, on which Bengt lay, behaved differently.

But on the morning watch it was fresh and fine. A feeling that we were beginning a new life filled us – a life shared with the sea.

Then we saw two cockroaches on the logs and sympathised with them.

They were in the same situation as we were but involuntarily. We called one Per and the other Lise.

LISE

PER

PER WAS AN UNLUCKY FELLOW AND TUMBLED OVERBOARD PRETTY SOON. BUT LISE WAS WITH US ALMOST THE WHOLE WAY TO POLYNESIA, TILL SHE PERISHED IN THE SAME TRAGIC MANNER. OUR OTHER FELLOW-PASSENGERS - BESIDES THE PARROT LORITA,- WERE CA. 1000 ANTS. THEY LIVED IN A CROSS-BEAM UNDER MY PILLOW. AND A FEW THOUSAND SHELL-FISH HELD ON TO THE LOGS IN THE CELLAR WITH THE HELP OF THEIR SUCKERS. THEY DEVELOPED COLOSSALLY AND THROVE EXCELLENTLY.

LORITA LOVED PENCILS. THIS IS MY LAST BUT ONE.

AN AMUSING GROUP OF PASSENGERS WERE A NUMBER OF PELAGIC CRABS IN THE TOURIST CLASS. THEY WERE OFTEN SITTING ON BIRDS' FEATHERS DRIFTING ON THE SEA, AND WHEN THEY CAUGHT SIGHT OF THE KON-TIKI, THEY JUMPED OVER TO US. ONE OF THE CRABS WE CALLED JOHANNES. HE LIVED IN A HOLE IN A LOG AFT AND WAS MORE THAN WILLING TO BE FED WITH SCRAPS OF BISCUIT. AT LAST HE BECAME SO ACCUSTOMED TO FINDING FOOD OUTSIDE HIS DOOR, THAT HE NO LONGER TROUBLED TO MOVE. HE GREW FAT AND LAZY, BUT WENT ASHORE IN POLYNESIA. THERE HE DIED, PERHAPS OF HUNGER.

FISH WERE ALREADY JUMPING HIGH ROUND THE VESSEL ON OUR FIRST DAYS IN THE HUMBOLDT CURRENT.

But soon we had something else to think about. For a time the wind and sea pretended not to see the curious insect. They left the impudent creature to the mercy of the

current, which does not care if one is a splinter or a big steamer. But then they perceived that the insect was in earnest. And so they set to work to shake it off.

The third night was the worst — then there was a struggle for life on the logs. The seas hurled themselves over the stern to smash the steering oar and carry away the two men who were on watch there. The steering oar of tough wood, as hard as iron, cracked, but nothing much more happened. Our raft behaved well. The water poured over it continually, but that did not matter, for there were holes in the bottom so that it ran out again just as quickly. The logs creaked and twisted each in its own way. The cabin swayed in one direction and the mast in another, rather as if the whole show were made of india-rubber. But the lashings held well. The bad weather had more effect on us. Our bodies ached and we got little sleep. Knut lay flat and green with seasickness.

Afterwards no one felt so much as a qualm. All things have an end — and so the dirty weather stopped being dirty and we felt we had everything very shipshape and pleasant.

The little cabin was better than the Bolivar in Lima itself, we thought. And here we need not put on suits and ties for meals either. At one end lay Herman, Thor, Bengt and I. Knut lay at our feet and at the other end lay Torstein with the wireless and Lorita.

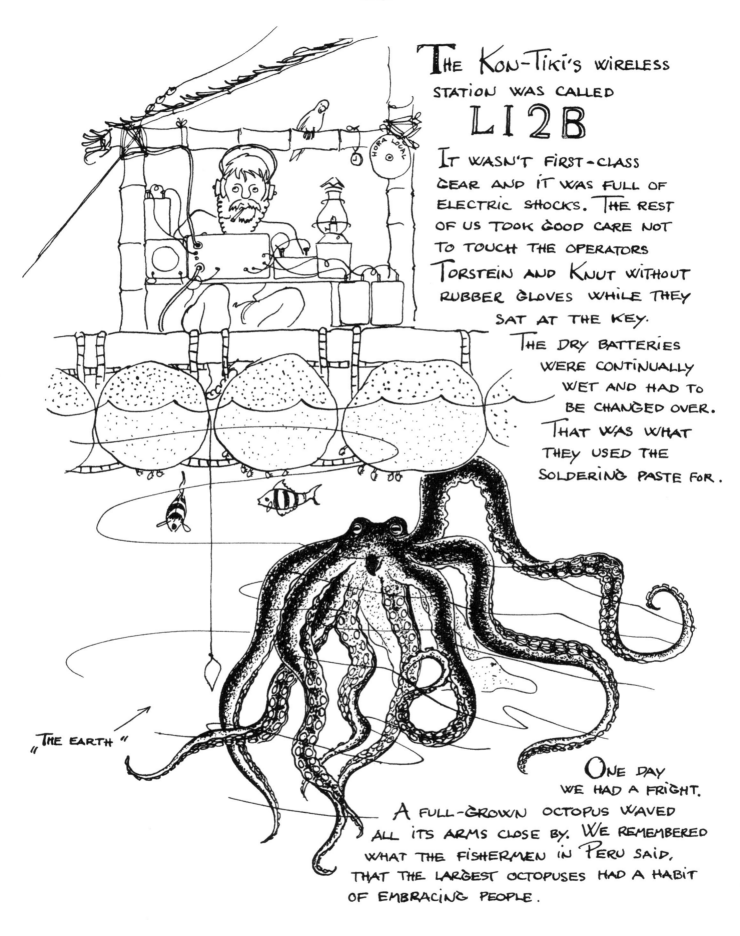

THE KON-TIKI'S WIRELESS STATION WAS CALLED **LI2B**
IT WASN'T FIRST-CLASS GEAR AND IT WAS FULL OF ELECTRIC SHOCKS. THE REST OF US TOOK GOOD CARE NOT TO TOUCH THE OPERATORS TORSTEIN AND KNUT WITHOUT RUBBER GLOVES WHILE THEY SAT AT THE KEY.

THE DRY BATTERIES WERE CONTINUALLY WET AND HAD TO BE CHANGED OVER. THAT WAS WHAT THEY USED THE SOLDERING PASTE FOR.

"THE EARTH"

ONE DAY WE HAD A FRIGHT. A FULL-GROWN OCTOPUS WAVED ALL ITS ARMS CLOSE BY. WE REMEMBERED WHAT THE FISHERMEN IN PERU SAID, THAT THE LARGEST OCTOPUSES HAD A HABIT OF EMBRACING PEOPLE.

The one we saw certainly did not care for us, for it did not attempt anything of the kind.

After 10 days the raft had drifted 500 sea miles in a north-westerly direction, through the cold green water of the Humboldt Current and out into the warm blue water of the real ocean.

And now the noblemen of the sea, the *Dolphins*, flocked about us. The dolphin is both nice to look at and nice to eat. It is the swiftest fish in the sea too, for it lives on

THE *Flying fish* AND SO HAS TO BE QUICK IN ITS MOVEMENTS.

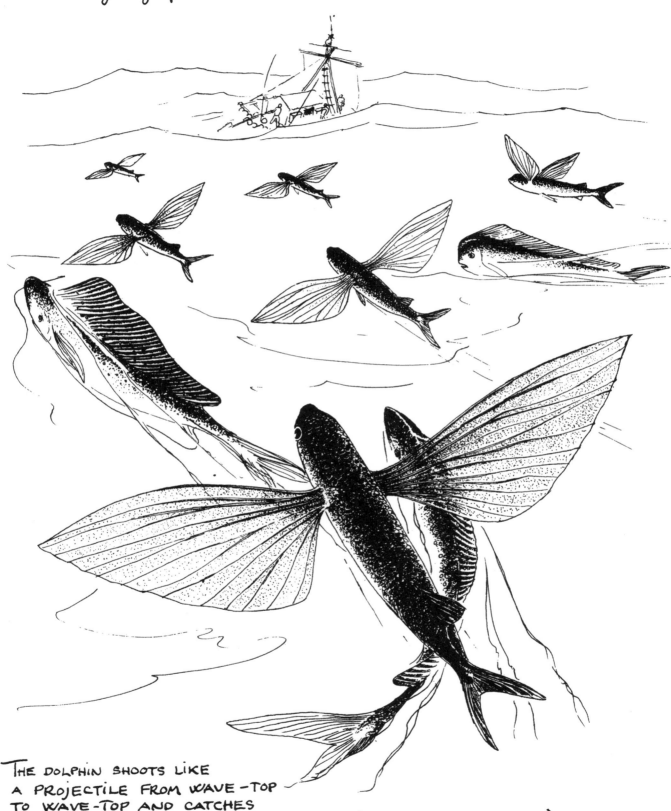

THE DOLPHIN SHOOTS LIKE
A PROJECTILE FROM WAVE-TOP
TO WAVE-TOP AND CATCHES
THE FLYING FISH WHEN THEY COME DOWN INTO THE WATER AGAIN.

THE DOLPHIN COULD CHANGE COLOUR TOO — FROM DEEP BLUE TO VIOLET, RED, YELLOW AND SILVERY WHITE. THEY COULD BE AS MUCH AS 5 FT. LONG, AND LIKED POTTERING ROUND THE RAFT AND RUBBING THEMSELVES AGAINST THE LOGS. THERE WERE SO MANY DOLPHINS ROUND THE RAFT ALL THE TIME THAT WE HAD ONLY TO FASTEN A HOOK TO A STICK, PUSH THE STICK DOWN INTO THE SCHOOL AND HAUL UP THE BEST AND BIGGEST.

FLYING FISH CAME SAILING THROUGH THE AIR IN SWARMS AND SMACKED AGAINST THE CABIN WALL. THE COOK'S FIRST JOB IN THE MORNING WAS TO COLLECT ALL THE FLYING FISH WHICH HAD COME ON BOARD IN THE NIGHT. ONE MORNING HERMAN FOUND 23. ONE FLYING FISH ALMOST HIT THE FRYING PAN.

BUT ONE NIGHT A NASTY SNAKE-LIKE FISH JUMPED RIGHT IN AT THE CABIN DOOR AND RIGHT DOWN INTO TORSTEIN'S SLEEPING BAG. THERE WAS A SHINDY IN THE DARK.

NO ONE COULD FIND THE LANTERN. SOON WE GOT HOLD OF THE SNAKE-FISH AND THEN A MAN'S LEG.

At last we caught the fish. It was greyish blue, about 3 ft. long and had teeth like a saw. We tried to find out what sort of a beast it was, but no description fitted it.

So we put the fish into a tin of formalin and took it with us to Polynesia. But no one there could tell us what kind of fish it was. We heard later that it was a Gempylus, and that no one had seen a live Gempylus before. Only skeletons had been found at one or two places in South America. So Torstein Raaby was presumably the first human being who had come in contact with a Gempylus — and that in an intimate manner, for it isn't every day one has a Gempylus in one's bed.

Up towards the Galapagos a big Turtle came floundering up to us. It looked good and we thought of turtle soup.

But the creature had no desire to become soup and paddled out of range as fast as possible.

There was no doubt now that we were going in the right direction. The S.E. trade wind blew surely and steadily.

The Kon-Tiki kept a good speed, now and then 2 sea miles an hour. We found that out by throwing a chip of wood into the water ahead of us and looking at a watch when the chip passed our stern. But across the ocean proper we kept a much higher speed - the South Equatorial Current saw to that. At noon every day the navigator — and that was I — drew a small circle on the chart, farther and farther away from South America. We could not do much to influence our course - the current and wind did that. We had only to fill the sail and keep the raft in her right position in relation to the seas.

The cabin had only one opening and we had to have that on the lee side so that the seas should not come in. But very often the raft twisted round and the sail kicked like a wild horse. Then all hands had to come on deck to hold the sail and row the vessel round. This took half an hour - she was so heavy. Sometimes we had to turn out 3-4 times on a dark night to struggle with the oar and hang on to the sail under the stars.

But we got accustomed to all this. Each man had 2 hours on watch and kept an eye on the course as well as he could, using an old boat's compass.

Time passed and beards grew
both on the raft and on ourselves.
A beard was pleasant to scratch.
I seemed to think so much
better then. Bengt had
the biggest and most stylish
beard — but on the top of
his head there was
not a single hair.
His hair grew
only under his
chin.

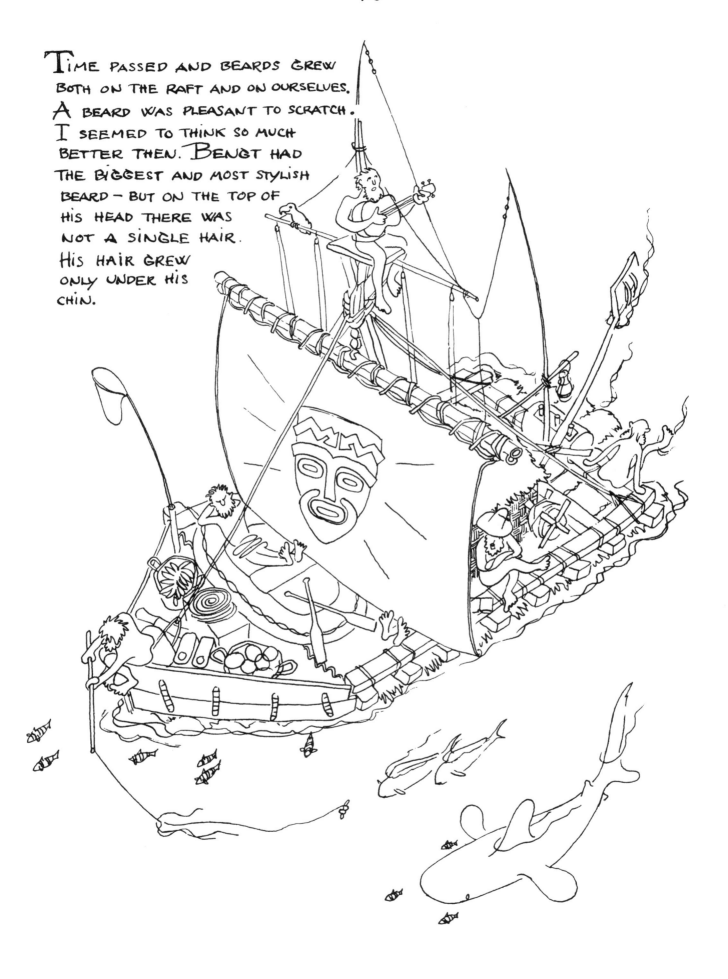

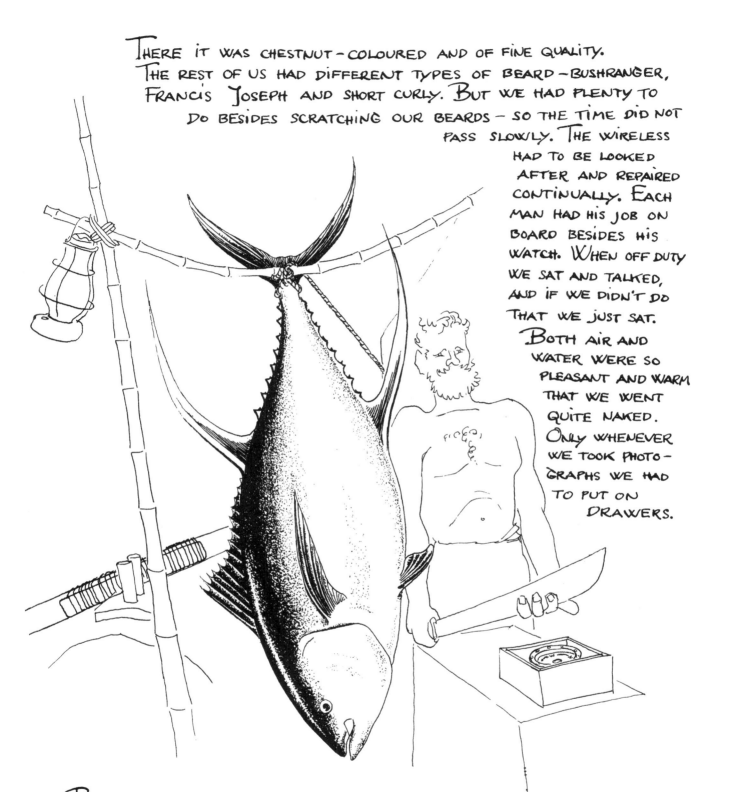

There it was chestnut-coloured and of fine quality. The rest of us had different types of beard — bushranger, Francis Joseph and short curly. But we had plenty to do besides scratching our beards — so the time did not pass slowly. The wireless had to be looked after and repaired continually. Each man had his job on board besides his watch. When off duty we sat and talked, and if we didn't do that we just sat. Both air and water were so pleasant and warm that we went quite naked. Only whenever we took photographs we had to put on drawers.

But sometimes we forgot the drawers — and so many yards of film were cut out when we got home — worse luck! And, well, we fished — and it was no small fry we hauled up. Here is Herman with a *Tunny*. It was so heavy that two men could only just carry it.

Sailfish we saw too, but they like a swiftly moving bait. We couldn't manage that with our old tub, so we left the sailfish in peace. But Sharks we caught, and plenty of them, 28 in all. They are greedy and strong, but easy to catch if the tackle is good. We had no proper shark hooks, only big cod hooks which we tied together and stuffed into a dolphin's stomach. We caught most of our sharks in this way. They came so near the raft that we could easily take hold of them. One morning 11 brown sharks were prowling round us: we hauled up 9 of them.

From the sharks we got our Pilot fish.

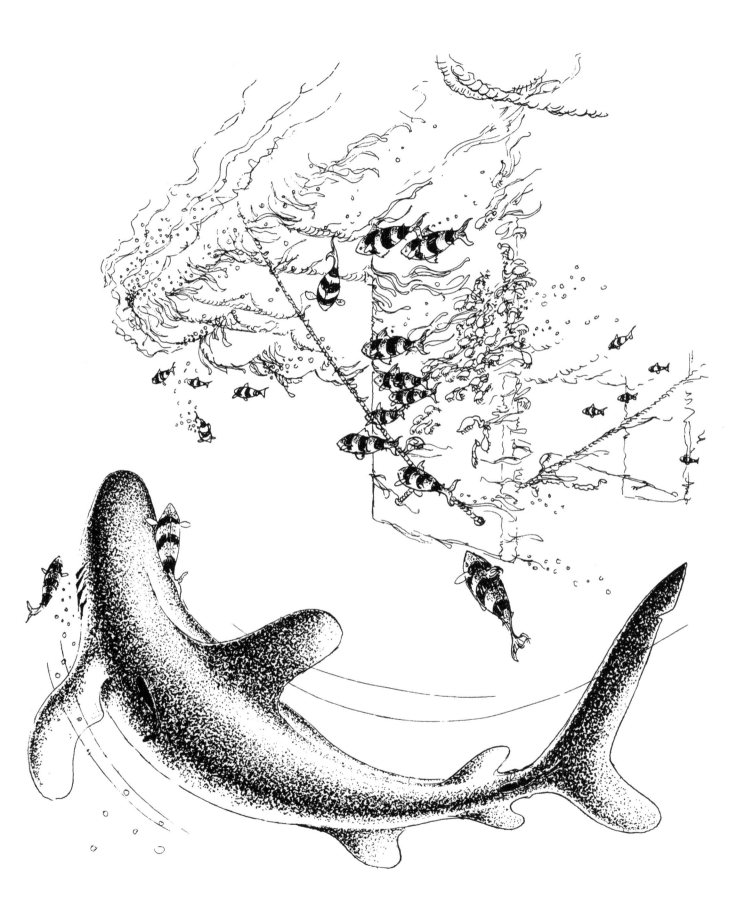

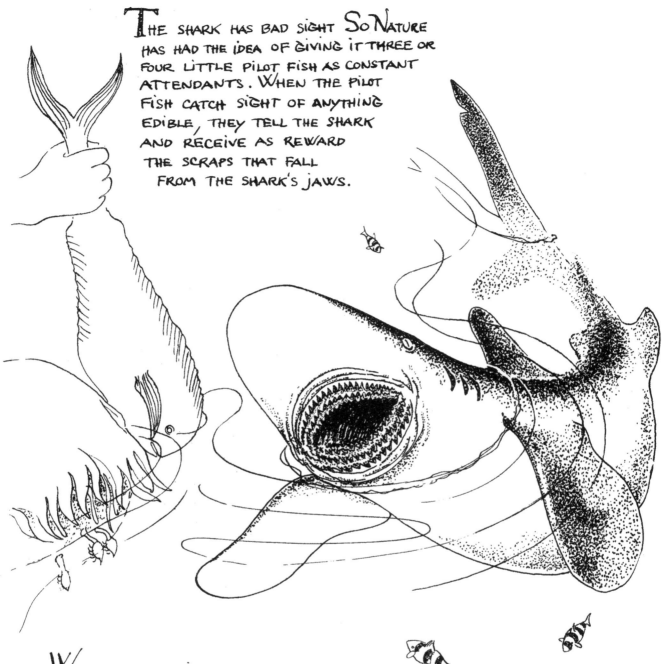

The shark has bad sight So Nature has had the idea of giving it three or four little pilot fish as constant attendants. When the pilot fish catch sight of anything edible, they tell the shark and receive as reward the scraps that fall from the shark's jaws.

When for the pilot fish the very basis of existence had disappeared, tail first, up on to the raft, they became unemployed and homeless. But then they thought that the raft was a ponderous shark and attached themselves to it, for a lot of eatables came out of the Kon-Tiki. As we neared Polynesia the queer flat raft-shark had at one time 60-70 pilot fish under the floor. We liked having the pilot fish and felt that they were our closest friends in the sea. Some of them swam 4000 sea miles on that occasion.

One day the world's biggest fish came
and sniffed at the KON-TIKI. That was a
sight we shall never forget. It was as improbable as the tallest story.

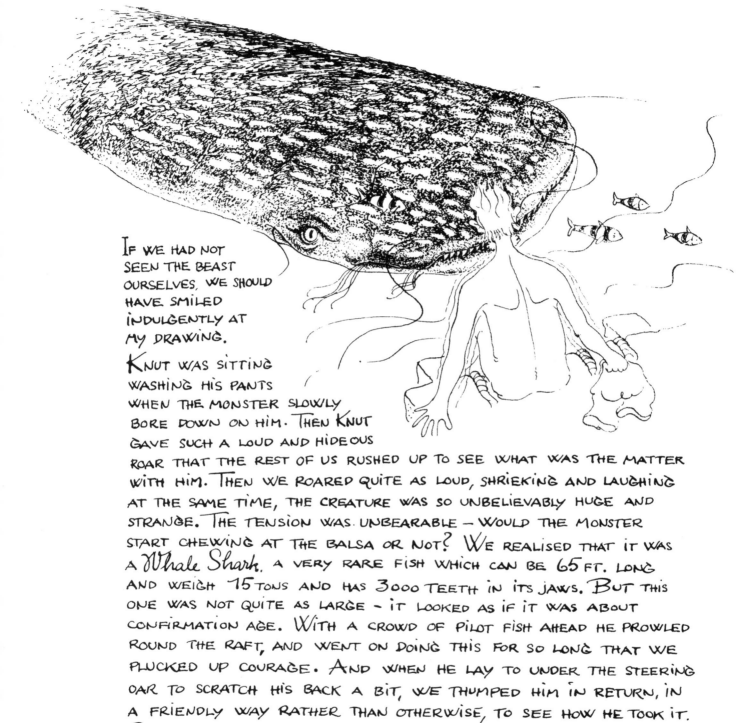

IF WE HAD NOT
SEEN THE BEAST
OURSELVES, WE SHOULD
HAVE SMILED
INDULGENTLY AT
MY DRAWING.

KNUT WAS SITTING
WASHING HIS PANTS
WHEN THE MONSTER SLOWLY
BORE DOWN ON HIM. THEN KNUT
GAVE SUCH A LOUD AND HIDEOUS
ROAR THAT THE REST OF US RUSHED UP TO SEE WHAT WAS THE MATTER
WITH HIM. THEN WE ROARED QUITE AS LOUD, SHRIEKING AND LAUGHING
AT THE SAME TIME, THE CREATURE WAS SO UNBELIEVABLY HUGE AND
STRANGE. THE TENSION WAS UNBEARABLE — WOULD THE MONSTER
START CHEWING AT THE BALSA OR NOT? WE REALISED THAT IT WAS
A *Whale Shark*, A VERY RARE FISH WHICH CAN BE 65 FT. LONG
AND WEIGH 15 TONS AND HAS 3000 TEETH IN ITS JAWS. BUT THIS
ONE WAS NOT QUITE AS LARGE — IT LOOKED AS IF IT WAS ABOUT
CONFIRMATION AGE. WITH A CROWD OF PILOT FISH AHEAD HE PROWLED
ROUND THE RAFT, AND WENT ON DOING THIS FOR SO LONG THAT WE
PLUCKED UP COURAGE. AND WHEN HE LAY TO UNDER THE STEERING
OAR TO SCRATCH HIS BACK A BIT, WE THUMPED HIM IN RETURN, IN
A FRIENDLY WAY RATHER THAN OTHERWISE, TO SEE HOW HE TOOK IT.
BUT HE LIKED IT AND CAME BACK AND LET HIMSELF BE THUMPED
THREE OR FOUR TIMES. THEN WE GAVE HIM A BIT OF A JAB WITH A
HARPOON, BUT WE OUGHT NOT TO HAVE DONE THAT, FOR HE DIDN'T LIKE
IT AND CLEARED OFF.
  A DAY OR TWO LATER WE HAD A STILL BIGGER FRIGHT, FOR WE
CAME NEAR BEING CAPSIZED BY *Whales* THE GIANTS OF THE SEA.
A LARGE SCHOOL OF THEM BORE STRAIGHT DOWN ON OUR LOGS, BLOWING.
WE LAY THERE IN THE MIDDLE OF THE TRAFFIC AND FELT LIKE A

WHEELBARROW IN NEW YORK. AND THEY DIDN'T KNOW ANYTHING
ABOUT KEEPING TO THE RIGHT EITHER. JUST AS THE BLOWHOLE OF
THE FIRST WAS ON A LEVEL WITH OUR PORT MAST, IT DIVED UNDER
THE RAFT WITH A GURGLE, AND ALL THE REST TOO, — LUCKILY.
WE DISTINCTLY FELT THE BACKWASH THEY MADE.

ONE REMAINED LYING UNDER THE RAFT TOO AND LOOKED LIKE A
GREAT BLACK SUBMERGED ROCK. ONCE TORSTEIN AND I SAW TWO
OF THE BIGGEST WHALES LEAP INTO THE AIR AND COME DOWN SMACK
ON THE WATER AGAIN WITH A TREMENDOUS SPLASH. THEN TORSTEIN
BURST INTO ROARS OF LAUGHTER, SO UNEARTHLY THAT I WAS QUITE
ANXIOUS ABOUT HIM.

IT IS CURIOUS TO THINK THAT GIGANTIC WHALES WEIGHING UP
TO 120 TONS LIVE ON MICROSCOPIC CREATURES. WE CAUGHT THESE
TOO. THEY ARE CALLED *Plankton* AND ARE FOUND IN GREAT
QUANTITIES IN ALL THE SEAS. WITH THE HELP OF A SMALL BAG-SHAPED
FINE-MESHED NET WE COULD GET MORE THAN 3 LBS. OF PLANKTON PER
HOUR IN SOME PLACES.

It looked like porridge, sometimes violet porridge and at other times like red porridge! Now and then we could make out the shape of individual creatures, such as these two.

One is a tiny little crab, the other is I don't know what — in any case it looked like its own X-ray photograph.

Then there was one which looked like a guitar with legs.

It was so big. The crab was a little bigger.

We tried to eat plankton too. It tasted like a mixture of stewed crab and wet paper, I thought.

We examined and collected in glass jars everything of zoological interest that we found. And to be able to contemplate submarine life without interference from sharks, we rigged up a diving basket of bamboo and ropes. We sat in this with spectacles on as long as our breath lasted. With the spectacles we could see as well under as above water.

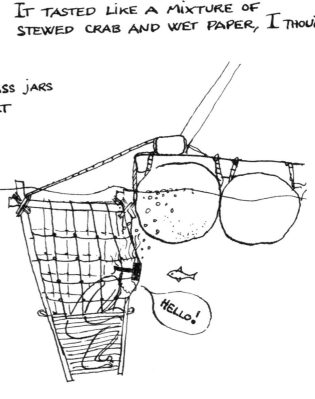

HELLO!

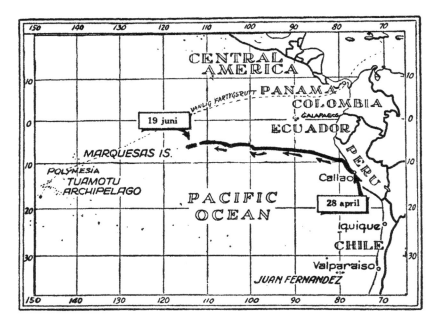

We had now been at sea nearly two months, and were more than halfway. The wind was more easterly. Each day carried us farther south, exactly as the current flowed. All hands were in good fettle; no one had even had as much as a fishbone in his throat. We never saw a ship, for there is no traffic. We might have been on another globe, utterly remote from the crazy world we came from.

Nor did we get bored with each other - on the contrary, we became like 6 brothers. The Kon-Tiki gave no trouble, and nor did we. If we felt an urge to be alone, we launched the rubber boat and

hung on a rope astern of the raft till we wanted company again.

We had food enough - tinned food and fish, cocoanuts and groats. But some little black insects lived in the groats, and they have been eating groats all the way from Peru. Steward Bengt Emmerik made two piles - one of groats and one of insects. It was a picture of the most profound peace.

We had brought drinking water from Peru in tins, and we collected rain water. Now and then it rained so violently that the air was as wet as the water. The things grew mouldy and I got rheumatism in my right leg.

Otherwise the sun rose and set, and nothing changed except our position on the globe. We saw no other sign of life above the water surface apart from ourselves and one or two jumping fish. We could not listen to the radio, to the news or the Norwegian fiddle – only short, concise telegrams referring to us.

On June 28th a wave washed over the logs and carried away Lorita. We could do nothing to save her. She must have been drowned at once, poor thing, or been taken by a shark. It was terribly sad, for we were all so fond of her. We only remember her good side – her infectious laughter, or when she tilted her head and said „Loriki" with which she meant Kon-Tiki. She was red and green like most parrots and was three and a half years old.

But a week later something happened which nearly cost a man his life. A breeze got up and Torstein's sleeping bag went overboard. Herman tried to catch the bag, but made a false step and he too tumbled into the sea. As the raft was making a good speed, it had passed before he could catch hold of it, and the steering oar was so covered with seawed and so slippery that he did not get a grip on that either. The whole thing happened so quickly that none of us could help.

There he lay astern in the middle of the Pacific, thousands of miles from the nearest land.

It was the worst thing that could happen, for the raft could not turn back – that was absolutely impossible! We had to act quickly before the sharks came. And Knut was the quickest. He flung out a lifebelt with a line, jumped into the sea and swam back to Herman with the lifebelt. He was only just in time, for Herman was already exhausted and a shark's fin was approaching - - -.

After this, we realised
that to fall overboard was the
most dangerous thing — that the Kon-Tiki
could face storms and great beasts, but
she could not pick up a man who lay in her wake.
Henceforward the man on watch was still more carefully
tethered to the vessel with a rope round his waist, on the principle
"Man overboard, overboard for good"

We were now drawing near to the Polynesian islands.
The weather was no longer so dependable. For a week the sail hung
down slack and the heat troubled us a bit. Then came the famous
small black cloud which grew bigger and bigger — and then we were
racing ahead in the storm under bare poles.

Suddenly a wall of rain burst upon us and pressed the sea flat. Only
the Kon-Tiki stood up against it like an old sodden barn in a meadow.
No sooner was the tap turned off than the wind rose again.

So it went on for many days. These were black spots in the sunny succession of days;

I only remember that my rheumatism was very active and that Herman crawled out with the anemometer from time to time and got 45 miles an hour.

We were very anxious now as to whether the Kon-Tiki would strike these small islands, for there was so much room on both sides.

But the current took us as we had calculated - straight down to the densest part of the Tuamoto group.

First we saw a solitary bird, and I am sure we never looked at a bird with greater interest. Then for a long time nothing happened, and we were tired of arguing as to who had seen the bird first, when a whole flock appeared.

And then one morning, after 93 days, we saw the eastern-most of the coral islands - Puka-Puka.

A low island lay to port, there was no doubt of that, and our reckoning said it was Puka-Puka, so there was no doubt either that we had reached Polynesia. Strangely enough most of us were not particularly excited about seeing land again. We could not get on shore anyway.

But Kon-Tiki just tumbled on westward with wind and current and did not care if there were ever so many Puka-Pukas in the neighbourhood. She would not let herself be manoeuvred to any island she did not want to go to herself. And Puka-Puka disappeared astern of us. But 3 days later we sighted another little coral island which was called Angatau.

We came so close to the island that we saw every coconut ashore, and got ready for stranding. But when there was only another 50 yards, the current carried us past the westernmost point and out to sea.

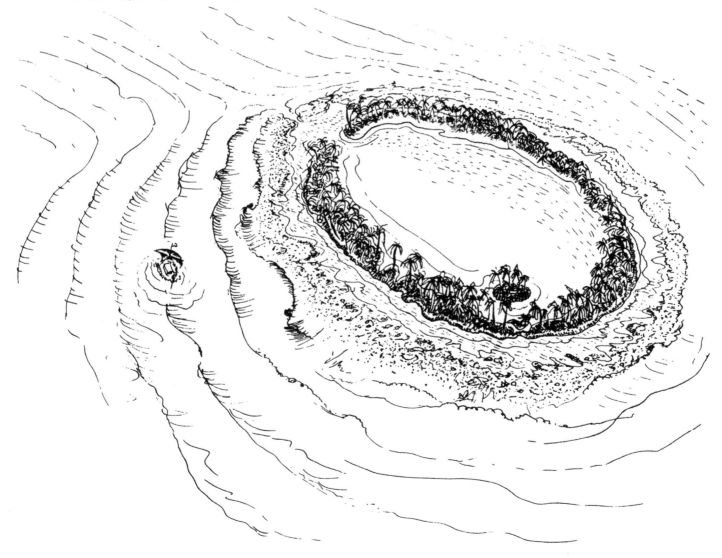

Just then a canoe came from the shore with two natives in it. "Good night," said one of them. This is fine, we thought, he speaks English, and asked what the island was called. "Good night," he said again. Then Torstein wanted to know how his mother was. As the answer to this too was "Good night", we realised that he was strong in English. But there was no time for more conversation, for the raft was slipping on. We hauled down the sail and rowed with all our might with a few small paddles we had with us. The two natives helped, and still

more canoes came and tried to tow the raft. But the raft would not be moved – no, to Angatau she would not go, though we kept on rowing till nearly midnight.

Knut had gone ashore with the rubber boat to get more help, and he only just managed to come aboard again before the light from the Kon-Tiki sank below the horizon to westward. So strong was the current and the way on the raft. Knut talked a lot about some fine hula girls on the island.

Our situation was not bright. All round lay low, treacherous coral reefs, so low that they cannot be seen till one is quite close to them. Current and wind, too, are constantly changing in these waters – among the most dangerous in the whole world. There we lay in a craft which drifted along, following her own head or that which was painted on the sail, and with no possibility of steering clear. On top of all this we had bad weather with violent rain squalls and a northerly breeze.

August 7th, 101 days from Peru, the voyage was over, for that morning the look-out shouted „ Land ahead!"

It must be Raroia, one of the larger islands. A look at the chart convinced us that it was. But how far off the island we were was not easy to say; Soon we saw palms all along the horizon to the westward and moved swiftly inshore towards them. Well, there was nothing else to do but make all clear for a landing through breakers and corals.

We hauled up the centreboards, lowered the sail and packed away the things we thought were important in waterproof bags. We continued to do this till the noise of the breakers filled the air. Then it was time to put our life-belts on our backs and our shoes on our feet.

The only chance we had was if we were able to cling to the logs as long as our strength lasted, and hope that the Kon-Tiki would be flung up on the reef.

So we stood by.

It looked ghastly, almost as if we should die then and there.

But before we had time to think any more about it, a wave came and heaved us right into the witches' cauldron. The raft gave a bump and a crack or two. Then we were drawn out again as if to take off for the next jump.

But a green wall of water, as clear as glass, with snow on the top, rose behind us and the next minute rushed down and buried the Kon-Tiki and all on board. Finally the mast snapped — the cabin collapsed and there was a smashing and twisting and crashing. But we were all alive, squeezed under the bamboos or clinging tight to ropes. Several waves of the same kind came until what was left of the raft was halfway up the reef.

Then we jumped down on to the red corals one by one and ran in across the reef to safety. And after us, in very truth, came the raft too, like a good-natured horse with Thor and Torstein on its back.

I can tell you that we were pleased with our raft. It had brought us to Polynesia with our lives and most of our equipment safe.

That Kon-Tiki, son of the sun, could have come to Polynesia in the same way, was quite certain.

We found the rubber boat
far in on the reef. It was punctured,
but we patched it and blew it up again for use in salvaging our things.
About 600 yards away, on the edge of the reef, lay a small island.
We floated our log book, water tins and provisions to it – and all the gear
we could move that day. We could not manage a great deal, for we
all had grazes and were pretty groggy. At last we could do no more
and threw ourselves down
on a green sward under
the palms.

The island was so small that we could go round it in five minutes.

There was no trace of people anywhere, nor on the neighbouring islands either.

The first thing we had to do now was to rig up a little wireless transmitter which had been salvaged and tell the outside world that we were alive on an uninhabited island on the Raroia Reef.

Just before we stranded Torstein had been in contact with a wireless fan on Rarotonga and told him that if he did not hear from us within 36 hours he was to notify our contacts in the U.S.A.

When 37 hours had passed the wireless still would not work and we thought we already heard the sound of aircraft in the distance.

But suddenly the operators got an answer to their signals from an amateur in Colorado, U.S.A., and from New Zealand.

Then they were not slow to report what had happened.

We waded to and fro between the raft and the island with things of all sorts. It was then we saw this queer fat fish.

It inflated itself when it was frightened to terrify its enemies by its appearance.

We saw a lot of snake-like
creatures on the reef and in
the lagoon as well.
They lay in heaps all
over the place and
wriggled. We paid no
particular attention
to them as we tramped
along. But later we heard
that they were a very
poisonous and fierce kind
of snake-fish called *Murenas*.
After a few days of hard
work we had settled in pretty
comfortably on the island with
our private house and bathing beach.
There was garden enough with coconut
palms and scented bushes. We thought this
must be Paradise and would have liked to stay
there for a long time. It was only the murena
that was the serpent in Paradise.

We dived in the lagoon with the submarine spectacles and saw a marvellously beautiful world. This drawing gives only a faint impression of it. There were corals which looked like petrified bunches of flowers – giant mussels with wavy mouths and fantastic fish which exceeded anything fantasy could invent.

There were swarms of hermit crabs and robber crabs on the island. The hermit crabs were so easy to catch that a moderate-sized cooking pot became full in no time. They were as red as a cooked lobster and as large as a man's fist. One night I woke with one hermit on my stomach and another on its way down into my sleeping bag.

Yes, it was indeed a good place, so peaceful and remote from the world, we thought.

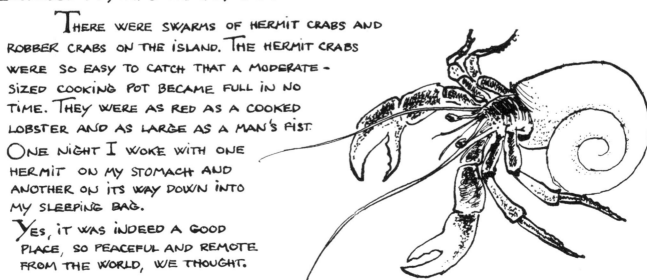

On the other side of the lagoon we could just see some other islands on the same reef.

After about a week had passed we perceived a sail crossing the lagoon towards us. We saw through the glasses that there were 3 men in a sailing canoe. Thor took our flag and waved it. The 3 in the boat waved back. When they waded ashore, they advanced with hands stretched out to show their friendliness. We said „Ia ora na", which means „good day" in Polynesian. Then they smiled all over and shouted „Ia ora na" in chorus. So now we were friends, and we said „Ia ora na" all that day and most of the next, for that was the only thing we could say in Polynesian.

Then another canoe came, and there was a chap in it who could talk a bit of French. We learned from him that there was a village on the other side and that they had found a box with „Kon-Tiki" on it over there. This „Tiki" had puzzled them very much in the village, as Tiki was their old god and someone had seen a light at night on that side of the lagoon where they never saw any lights.

But at last they had overcome their fear and here they were.

We agreed with the natives that Bengt as our envoy, should go over to the village with the canoes. Next day he came back with the chief himself, who was called Teka.

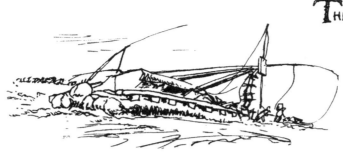

THE CHIEF WAS A STOUT FELLOW. HE KNEW QUITE A LOT AND REALISED THAT WE WERE NOT SHIPWRECKED SAILORS, BUT A KIND OF EXPEDITION WHICH HAD SOMETHING TO DO WITH TIKI.

THE CHIEF BROUGHT WITH HIM THE WHOLE MALE PART OF THE POPULATION. THEY WERE TREMENDOUSLY INTERESTED IN ALL THE STRANGE GEAR WE HAD. THE WIRELESS IN PARTICULAR THEY THOUGHT WAS GREAT FUN.

AND WHEN KNUT MANAGED TO GET SOMEONE WHO WAS HAVING A TALK, THEIR JUBILATION WAS IMMENSE, THOUGH THE JARRING AND SQUEAKING WERE SOMETHING AWFUL.

THEN THE WHOLE CROWD, WITH THE CHIEF AND OURSELVES AT THE HEAD, WADED OUT ON THE REEF TO SEE THE STRANGEST THING OF ALL — OUR RAFT.

THEY WERE GREATLY ASTONISHED AND THERE WAS A LOT MORE TALK ABOUT TIKI. THEY POINTED TO THE LOGS AND TO THE BREAKERS, AND SHOOK THEIR HEADS - - - - -

THE CHIEF TEKA WANTED US TO COME OVER TO HIS VILLAGE AS GUESTS.

WE HAD NO OBJECTION TO THIS AND SET ABOUT MOVING OUR THINGS ACROSS THE LAGOON IN CANOES.

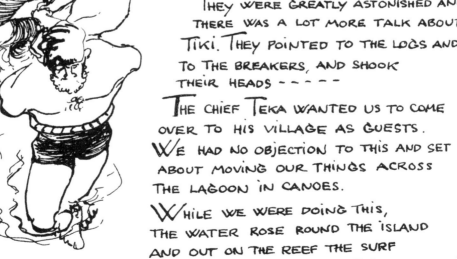

POLYNESIAN FISH HOOK

WHILE WE WERE DOING THIS, THE WATER ROSE ROUND THE ISLAND AND OUT ON THE REEF THE SURF THUNDERED AS NEVER BEFORE.

IT WAS TOO MUCH FOR THE RAFT TOO. IT BUTTED ITS WAY FORWARD, MAKING FOR THE ISLAND, IN A WAY IT WAS A PLEASURE TO SEE. WE STOOD BY WITH ROPES

AND CAUGHT HOLD
OF IT. WHEN IT WANTED
TO MOVE OUT INTO THE LAGOON,
WE MANAGED AFTER MUCH EFFORT
TO MAKE IT FAST TO A PALM TRUNK.

OVER IN THE VILLAGE THERE WAS AN AIR
OF WELL-BEING. ALL WHO COULD WALK OR CRAWL
HAD COME TO MEET US.

THE WOMEN STOOD IN READINESS WITH WREATHS OF FLOWERS
AND HUNG THEM ROUND OUR NECKS. WE FELT A BIT EMBARRASSED
WHEN THEY STUCK FLOWERS ALL OVER US — BEHIND OUR EARS
AND IN OUR BEARDS. BUT THAT IS POLYNESIAN CUSTOM,
SO THERE IS NOTHING STRANGE IN IT.

ONE OF THE LADIES LED US OFF TO A HUT AND
THERE LAY A LITTLE BOY WHO LOOKED VERY ILL.
HE HAD A NASTY BOIL ON HIS HEAD. WE UNDER-
STOOD THAT THE LADY WAS THE BOY'S MOTHER
AND WANTED US TO ATTEND HIM.

KNUT HAD A LITTLE EXPERIENCE OF SUCH
THINGS FROM WAR-TIME, AND WASHED
THE BOIL WITH BORACIC.

We now found good use for our medicine chest from the Kon-Tiki, for they had neither doctor or medicine on the island.

In the evening they arranged a great feast at which we were guests of honour. While we sat and ate roast sucking pig, breadfruit and chicken, the young girls danced round us. It was not the kind of dancing to which we were accustomed. No, they stood with their arms over their heads and wriggled their backsides rapidly. But it wasn't so easy for us to eat properly while this sort of thing was going on.

When at last we had eaten our fill, the whole village sat down in a circle and the great dance began. Some of them played on a sort of guitar

and others sang. For a time nothing else happened. But then the music grew livelier and soon a young hula girl leapt into the ring and wriggled. She stopped in front of Herman.

It was clear

that she liked him and wanted him to dance with her.

But Herman was not very keen as the two of them were to dance alone, as is the custom in Polynesia.

But she would not give way, and the rest of us naturally shouted to him not to be afraid and we teased him so long that he had no choice but to fling himself into a wild serpentine dance which left him quite blown.

We laughed till we lay flat on our backs,

"Hula Thor"

We used to wander about with the children looking at queer shells.

But we ought not to have done so, for now one girl after another came and wriggled invitingly before us too. And of course we couldn't be less than Herman.

It was a bad show. Even I who was rheumatic and sat in my sheepskin trousers to warm up the rheumatism had to step forward.

I wriggled till my carcase creaked and invented every figure imaginable. It was certainly very funny to watch, because there was a rent in the back of my skin trousers and a strip of skin with fur on it, hung out, just like a rabbit's scut.

At last there was no more music, only a queer sort of panting and groaning, so that the girl and I had to stop to see what it was.

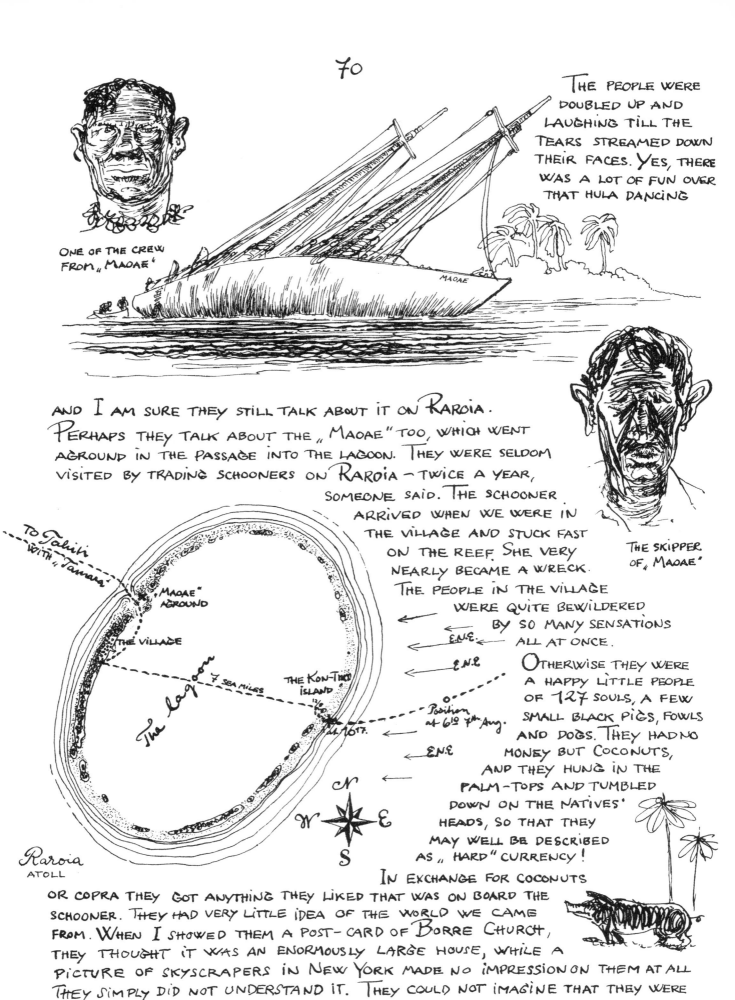

ONE OF THE CREW FROM "MAOAE"

THE PEOPLE WERE DOUBLED UP AND LAUGHING TILL THE TEARS STREAMED DOWN THEIR FACES. YES, THERE WAS A LOT OF FUN OVER THAT HULA DANCING

THE SKIPPER OF "MAOAE"

AND I AM SURE THEY STILL TALK ABOUT IT ON RAROIA. PERHAPS THEY TALK ABOUT THE "MAOAE" TOO, WHICH WENT AGROUND IN THE PASSAGE INTO THE LAGOON. THEY WERE SELDOM VISITED BY TRADING SCHOONERS ON RAROIA — TWICE A YEAR, SOMEONE SAID. THE SCHOONER ARRIVED WHEN WE WERE IN THE VILLAGE AND STUCK FAST ON THE REEF. SHE VERY NEARLY BECAME A WRECK. THE PEOPLE IN THE VILLAGE WERE QUITE BEWILDERED BY SO MANY SENSATIONS ALL AT ONCE.

OTHERWISE THEY WERE A HAPPY LITTLE PEOPLE OF 127 SOULS, A FEW SMALL BLACK PIGS, FOWLS AND DOGS. THEY HAD NO MONEY BUT COCONUTS, AND THEY HUNG IN THE PALM-TOPS AND TUMBLED DOWN ON THE NATIVES' HEADS, SO THAT THEY MAY WELL BE DESCRIBED AS "HARD" CURRENCY!

IN EXCHANGE FOR COCONUTS

To Tahiti with "Tamara"

"MAOAE" AGROUND

THE VILLAGE

The Lagoon

7 SEA MILES

THE KON-TIKI ISLAND

Position at 6⁰⁰ 7ᵗʰ Aug.

E.N.E.

Raroia ATOLL

OR COPRA THEY GOT ANYTHING THEY LIKED THAT WAS ON BOARD THE SCHOONER. THEY HAD VERY LITTLE IDEA OF THE WORLD WE CAME FROM. WHEN I SHOWED THEM A POST-CARD OF BORRE CHURCH, THEY THOUGHT IT WAS AN ENORMOUSLY LARGE HOUSE, WHILE A PICTURE OF SKYSCRAPERS IN NEW YORK MADE NO IMPRESSION ON THEM AT ALL THEY SIMPLY DID NOT UNDERSTAND IT. THEY COULD NOT IMAGINE THAT THEY WERE HOUSES TOO.

Knut and Herman succeeded in curing the sick boy with the help of the penicillin brought from the Kon-Tiki. They wirelessed to Los Angeles and consulted a doctor as well. All this made an enormous impression on the natives.

Not least when we distributed provisions and empty water tins from the Kon-Tiki. Then enthusiasm knew no bounds.

A few days before our departure we were ceremonially admitted into the tribe and received Polynesian names. Thor's name on Raroia is: Varoa Tikaroa; Herman's is Tupuhoe-Itetahua; Bengt's is Topakino; Knut's is Tefaunui; Torstein's is Maroake and my name is Tane-Maturau. These were all names taken from Polynesian history and legend and good names to have.

We now learned by wireless that the French Government schooner "Tamara" was on her way from Tahiti to fetch us on orders from Paris. And one day "Tamara" came with cinema men and the administrator of the Tuamoto islands, Monsieur Frédéric Ahnne, on board. When the administrator saw the raft, he wanted to tow it right to Tahiti. It was a sad good-bye to the natives on Raroia.

Tahiti

WE HAD BECOME FOND OF THEM AND THEY OF US.
AS THEY STOOD THERE IN A LITTLE BUNCH AND SANG A LAST FAREWELL
SONG, IT MUST BE OWNED THAT EACH OF US HAD A LUMP IN HIS THROAT.

THE „TAMARA" WAS QUITE AN ORDINARY SCHOONER
WITH A MOTOR WHICH
SAID „ PAPA, MAMMA,
PAPA, MAMMA,
PAPA,
MAMMA,
PAPA,
MAMMA"
ALL THE WAY
TO TAHITI

Papeete
Tahiti

IN PAPEETE
THERE WERE GREAT
DOINGS AND IMITATION
HULA GIRLS WITH FLOWERS.
WE PLANTED IN THE
GOVERNOR'S GARDEN
A COCONUT WHICH WE HAD
BROUGHT WITH US FROM PERU.
TODAY IT IS A LITTLE PALM 8 FT. TALL.

There is not much left of the South Seas paradise in Papeete. There are big cars, cinemas, bars. Galvanised iron and chewing gum, but it isn't so bad there all the same. My rheumatism was worse though, — so bad that I had to have treatment. I wondered if Kon-Tiki had got rheumatism too after his raft trip 1500 years ago, — tradition says nothing about it.

Some people said it was lumbago while others said it was sciatica — it was painful anyway.

There was only one person in Papeete who could cure my leg and that was Monsieur Milette. With massage and one thing and another, they said, he had cured many people who were much worse than me.

Well, Monsieur Milette came. He was a little mild man with a curious long nose. He tackled the rheumatism with tremendous energy. But he didn't want any money, he said. If I could help him to become a good clown for the Tahiti amateur competition for the best comic turn, we should be quits.

I felt this was a genuine offer, for he was good material to make a clown of.

First he massaged me till I creaked. But that did no good. Then he tried electric shocks, but that did no good either.

Then, he said, the only thing which will do any good is "Chinese nails", and he stuck some long silver nails into my leg at various "strategic" points.

But the Chinese method, too, made me no better. Finally he pulled over my head a canvas bag with a hole in it and lit a Primus under me — — — — Then it was time to make a clown of him. I gave him a longer nose, bushy eyebrows and bigger ears. He borrowed my sheepskin trousers and went off to the competition.

Altogether there were three clowns competing. When Monsieur Milette saw them, he became so nervous that he couldn't say anything funny and unfortunately finished third. It wasn't my fault!

I still had my beard. It was a queer beard —

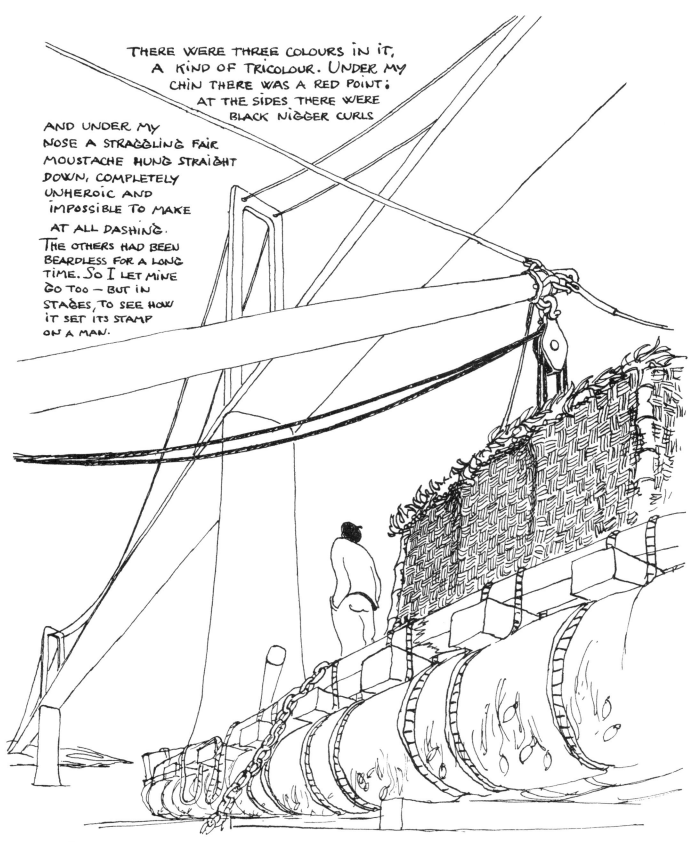

THERE WERE THREE COLOURS IN IT, A KIND OF TRICOLOUR. UNDER MY CHIN THERE WAS A RED POINT; AT THE SIDES THERE WERE BLACK NIGGER CURLS

AND UNDER MY NOSE A STRAGGLING FAIR MOUSTACHE HUNG STRAIGHT DOWN, COMPLETELY UNHEROIC AND IMPOSSIBLE TO MAKE AT ALL DASHING. THE OTHERS HAD BEEN BEARDLESS FOR A LONG TIME. SO I LET MINE GO TOO — BUT IN STAGES, TO SEE HOW IT SET ITS STAMP ON A MAN.

WE WERE ON TAHITI A GOOD, LONG TIME WAITING FOR A PASSAGE TO THE U.S.A. AT LAST LARS CHRISTENSEN'S BOAT "THOR I" CAME TO PAPEETE SPECIALLY AND TOOK US OFF. THE KON-TIKI TOO, WAS STOWED ON BOARD THE "THOR I" AND AFTER A VOYAGE OF 10 DAYS WE PASSED THE GOLDEN GATE BRIDGE INTO SAN FRANCISCO.

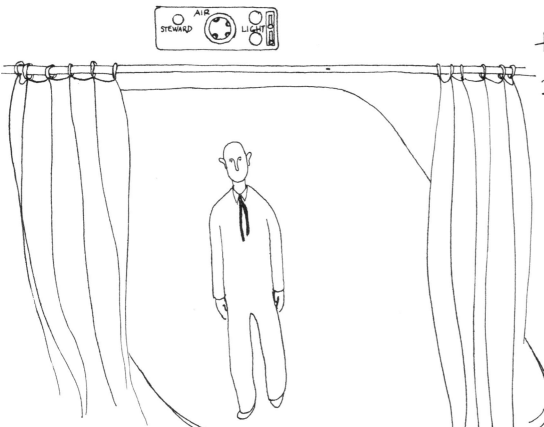

HERE WE SAID GOOD-
BYE TO BROTHER
BENGT, WHO WAS
GOING TO SEATTLE
TO STUDY.
HE STOOD ON THE
AIRFIELD A LONELY
FIGURE –
WITHOUT US,
WITHOUT HAIR,
AND WITHOUT
BEARD.
HIS FINE BEARD
HAD BEEN LEFT
ON RAROIA.

THE KON-TIKI LAY IN SAN FRANCISCO
HARBOUR WAITING FOR DECK
SPACE TO NORWAY,
WHILE WE FLEW TO
WASHINGTON.

WE HAD A LOT OF FUN
THERE TOO.
WE WERE AT THE PRESIDENT'S.
HE POINTED TO A GLOBE
AND SAID „THAT'S WHERE YOU'VE
SAT ON A RAFT FOR 101 DAYS".
„YES", SAID WE. „THAT'S 100 DAYS
MORE THAN I'D HAVE LIKED TO SIT
ON A RAFT," SAID THE PRESIDENT.

THEN WE FLEW HOME TO NORWAY AND
I TRAVELLED BY THE OLD VESTFOLD RAILWAY
TO BORRE STATION. THERE STOOD
GUNDERSEN AND HIS WIFE, LISS AND
ANNE KARIN, THE TWO BILLES,
LILA AND HANS, WHO OWN
SOLBAKKEN AND SEVERAL
MORE.

ANNE KARIN
HAD GROWN
SO BIG.

THE COCK AND HENS
WERE IN
GLASS BOTTLES.

AND PIUS HAD HAD
A SON. IN THE
GARDEN I SAW THE
ENDS OF BOTH OF
THEM – – –

– –AND THE END OF MY JOURNEY.

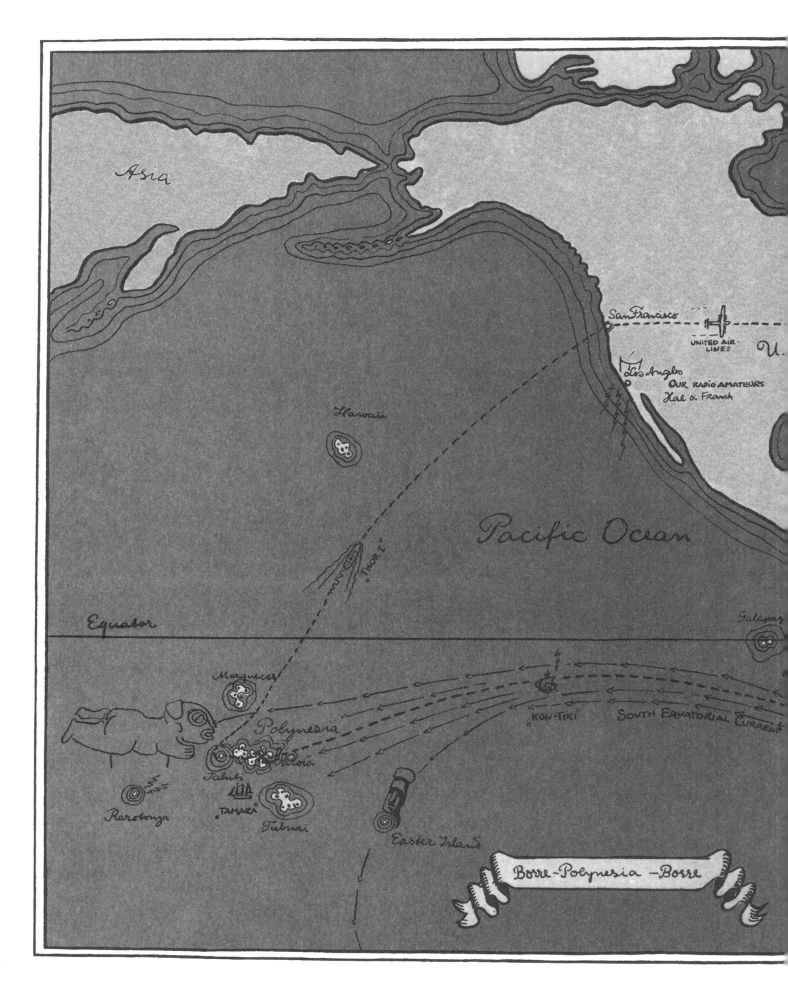

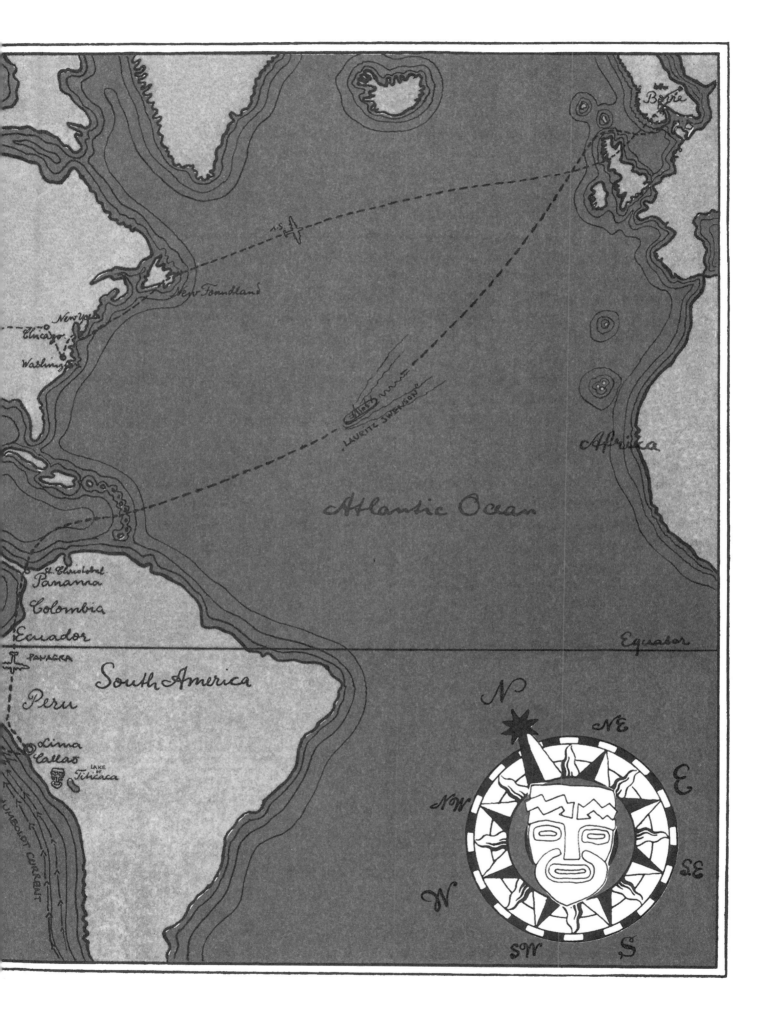